Lynn Ferguson

NOTES FROM THE VALLEY

Ferdle LLC
5632 Van Nuys Blvd, Unit 3083
Sherman Oaks, Los Angeles,
California, USA 91401
www.YouTellYours.com

This book is dedicated to

Mark, Fergus and Lachlan

where all my stories begin and end.

INTRODUCTION

Whether you like it or not, Sundays can be the trickiest days of the week.

Fridays bring the promise of the weekend, and letting loose. Saturdays are all about hanging out or shopping, going to watch movies, or the theatre, or kicking back in front of the telly with something sugary or something with alcohol content.

And then the clock hits midnight, and Sunday appears with all of its judgment and wholesome expectations.

Glorious, carefree, and seemingly endless, or just as easily miserable, claustrophobic, and seemingly endless, there's something about a Sunday where there's always some moment when you find yourself reflecting on where your life is currently going.

Like I say, as days of the week go, Sundays are potentially tricky.

When I was a kid, I used to spend my Sundays moaning about the existence of Mondays. Because obviously nobody loves a Monday when that means going to school.

Once I hit adolescence, I'd developed this basic moaning into a great manifesto about how nobody understood me anyhow and how life was unfair, because it was almost a whole entire other week of school until Friday.

But later when I worked in stand-up comedy, I absolutely loved Sundays. They were days to travel back home from out-of-town gigs or mooch around the sofa in pajamas, bleary-eyed and happily worse for wear after the Thursday to Saturday late-night shifts and jobs well -or not so well- done. Occasionally I would do laundry. More often, I would not. Friends might come over. Carbs would be consumed. We'd laugh and talk about what had just been, and what would be at play in the upcoming week.

When I had young kids, Sundays were days to take them to the park, to get laundry done, to cook a roasted something with potatoes and vegetables. I'd potter around checking school notifications and to check they'd caught up on school work. I'd smile when my kids moaned about the upcoming Monday, remembering the days when I used to moan that way about Mondays too.

And through all these variations of my Sundays, one thing remained the same: I used to phone my Mum back in Scotland to give her an update on life.

When I left home, it was the one thing she made me promise to do.

Now, here's where I'm meant to tell you that those phone calls were the most important conversations I had in my life and that I cherished every one, but that would not be true. The world is a big and busy place and trying to make sure that I got a phone call through to Cumbernauld, Scotland for 2 pm local time on a Sunday wasn't always easy to navigate.

But if you'd met my Mum, you'd have worked out a way to navigate it too.

So, I'd call her from Australia or Hong Kong, navigating stupid time differences. Or lift the phone bleary-eyed, after having been up too late doing stuff on Saturday that my Mum really didn't need to know about. There were times I'd have a snarly baby on my hip and a kid running up and down the hallway yelling Power Rangers Lightspeed Rescue, and the washing machine might have broken or a car alarm might be going off, and I'd still have to assure her that even though I might sound 'a little down' my frustrations were only temporary and life really was, on the whole, just fine.

Truthfully, I didn't always relish the calls. My Mum could have been a brilliant interrogator because she always had a way of making you talk, and I didn't always want to talk. But I loved her, and respected her, and would call her every Sunday.

Then the calls stopped. She died on December 1st, 2008 and so I didn't call her anymore.

Now, I'm a big old grown woman and I am used to missing my mum. I don't like it, but I accept that it's part of life. People die and it hurts. And it really hurts when it's people you really love. But part of being a grown-up is accepting parts of life you don't particularly like, so I got on with things.

Then one Sunday in November 2022, I found myself with a weird sense of lostness - like I'd left the kettle on, or left a tap running, or forgotten something. It wasn't grief - I know what grief feels like. It was something else. And it wasn't just because it was Sunday and everybody can get out of whack on a Sunday.

So when I stopped to think about what was bothering me, I realized that I missed the way I used to feel about the world when I used to call my Mum: That there was an order to things: That even when I didn't particularly know where I was going, the world was a good place, where scary things happen from time to time, but mostly everything turns out alright.

And I wasn't sure I felt that anymore.

And then I argued with myself that the whole idea of this loss was just bullshit. The world has always been mental. The whole timeline of history is full of people being mental. And sometimes you just miss people, that's all. And it sucks that people die, but they do. And Sundays just can be the trickiest days of the week.

But then I argued back (because I am good at that) that the past ten years in the world have been full-on. Not just for me but for everyone. And even if my mother were alive to hear what had been happening, she would be uncharacteristically speechless at the extent of it all.

And yet, in the middle of all of this, I would want to tell her how there were still really good people, doing really good things. And that I still thought the world was kind of beautiful. And that in times when I was living through my greatest uncertainty, I hadn't lost the ability or desire to laugh.

I thought about how one Sunday in 2020 when the whole world was in lockdown, my eldest had announced with a sigh, "Who knew that living through a major historical event could be so completely tedious?" and we'd laughed about the silliness and yet complete sense of his comment for weeks. And I knew she would have laughed too.

I'm not sure if it was what my Mum told me, or what I was telling her that made me feel like there was a steady beat to life, but I wanted it back. Though my younger self would be screaming at me in disbelief, I wanted the structure back.

So I figured I would take that time that I used to call my Mum and send a note about what's been going on in my week into the Universe instead.

So I did.

Almost straight away, people started writing back, because it turns out I'm not the only person who feels a bit reflective on a Sunday.

So I wrote more notes. And more people wrote back. And now a note goes out every Sunday at exactly the same time that I used to call my Mum - which because I live in the San Fernando Valley in California, and she lived in Cumbernauld Scotland means it is 6:01am my time. (She would so approve of the inconvenience.)

It's not the same as calling my Mum, because nobody can grill me quite as effectively about my health/haircut/weight/happiness as she could, and because she herself is irreplaceable.

But I have found in writing these Notes from the Valley what I felt I lost.

The world is a good place, where scary and sometimes pretty horrific things happen, but it's still kind of beautiful.

This book is a collection of all of those notes I've sent out on a Sunday for this past year. The year spans November to November rather than January through December because I started in November and because real life is messy.

They are sent with love and with gratitude for your existence, wherever in the world you find yourself placed.

You can follow to get the latest notes at www.lynnfergy.com

TABLE OF CONTENTS

Introduction

Table of Contents

About the Author

Nov 20, 2022

THE WHY AND THE WHERE

Landing

I've been thinking for a while that I need to perk up my Sundays. Here in Tweddley Manor, Sundays generally involve laundry, cleaning up, negotiating feathery politics between the chickens, or periodically persuading my 15-year-old that homework really isn't against the rules of the Geneva Convention.

It wasn't always this way. I used to phone my mother every Sunday. It was one of her 'suggestions'. And if you ever met my mother, you'd know that when she had a 'suggestion', you should follow it.

After meeting my mother, Mark named her Don Fergusoni - the family boss who could control everything without even getting up from her chair.

So, from the day I left home at 18 and moved into my first apartment, I'd find time every Sunday to make the call.

Over the years, I've called her from Hong Kong, from Australia, and most of Europe and obviously here in America, navigating a plethora of bloody timezones in the way. As a result, I can translate 2pm in Cumbernauld, Scotland to virtually any other time zone on the planet.

A mother to four children and a schoolteacher, she could have been an interrogator because there was nothing she could not find out. She could smell a lie like a sniffer dog can find cocaine.

But we talked freely. We fought, we argued, we discussed, we laughed, we conspired, we connected. She drove me absolutely fucking crazy, but I still knew I was lucky.

And time passed and we all got older and after a marriage of almost 50 years, my mum was widowed. Her arthritis took firm hold, and brought the gateway to other illnesses.

By then I lived 500 miles away, and phoning her on a Sunday became less about stopping her worrying and more about stopping my own.

I was offered a job in LA in 2008 and my mother was determined I should take it. By then she was in hospice care and I didn't want to be 5000 miles away.

"You have one life. Have it."

So, in October 2008, Mark and I arrived in the country with 8 suitcases and two children under the age of 6.

My mother thought it was thrilling - so exciting in fact, she enjoyed a call once a day on my way to work. And also on a Sunday.

On the 1st of December 2008, less than two months after I arrived in the San Fernando Valley, my mother died.

I was bereft, but life was busy. And I was two other people's mother. So, I put my head down and set to work.

And so many Sundays passed.

Sometimes I don't think about it. Other Sundays I find myself pottering about like I've forgotten something. I miss her, obviously, and always always will. But I miss what she showed me - that taking time to reflect on how you see simple things is how to really connect to life

So I figured that maybe, amongst doing the laundry, navigating dogs, chickens and teenagers, I could write these "Notes from The Valley" and send them out on a Sunday.

They're not addressed to my mother, because that frankly would be creepy. Besides, I figure if I just make them truthful, Don Fergusoni would find a way to see them.

THANKSBRINGING

T day

It was Thanksgiving in the US this week. As a Scot, it's not really my holiday, and also - no offense Americans - it doesn't historically seem to be something I'd really want to be celebrating.

It's a bit like Guy Fawkes night in the UK. Ok so everybody likes a rebel, but the whole idea of it was a bit gory and the fact was that Guy Fawkes bloody hated Scottish people, gives me the sense we'd hate each other. A tricky thing about life is learning to choose our heroes wisely.

Anyway, back to the point. Because Thanksgiving isn't really our holiday, it takes the pressure off.

We don't have turkey - because we have that at Christmas. And the boys are not fans of pumpkin pie - so we have cake. But we do acknowledge the occasion by sitting round a table.

We eat food from all around the world, Pernil from Puerto Rico, Indian pakora, pumpkin bread, Mutabal Shawander made with Beets from the backyard, potatoes from everywhere, Mac and cheese - from wherever Mac and cheese comes from - because you can present whatever fancy dish you want to my youngest, but if pasta and cheese aren't involved, he doesn't care.

I don't have lovely Thanksgiving ware from a posh shop. Instead it's served up in a couple of random dishes I have left from my mother's 'good' dinner set. They have sunflowers on them because it was the 70s, but they conveniently also work for Thanksgiving. The table is set with a frankly frickin' beautiful quilted table runner made by Mark's mum - with turkeys with tartan wings. The people around the table, are perfectly imperfect individuals who I'm grateful are alive.

I grew up thinking gratitude was the same as smugness. I certainly had a weird perception of it. If I said I was really grateful for something as a kid, it was only a matter of time before some other kid broke it. Women who said they were grateful for their wonderful husbands tended to be divorced within the year. So it was something I avoided.

But there's something to this thankfulness. Just taking a break to look around and say, "This is alright" wherever the 'this' happens to be, seems like a good idea.

When I look back at my life, too much of it has been based on what I didn't get right: Too much information was about how to improve, or how I wasn't there yet. I was too thin, too fat, too old, too boring, too intense, too foolish, too fucking blah blah blah (insert personal word of choice). It's endless.

But what if, for one day, everything is completely alright as it is? What a fucking relief. How about putting your foot on the brake and taking the foot off the self-criticism or fear for the future for a while? It doesn't have to be over a turkey or a Thanksgiving table - though in this house it probably involves the obligatory Mac and cheese.

No single thing is responsible for my happiness or my unhappiness. It's the combination of many things. And sometimes I get so busy I forget.

So I will take your Thanksgiving, Americans. I'm not in with the history per se. But I like the focus. That there's always something to be grateful for, even on those days when it's hard to see.

Peace and love.

Dec 4, 2022

ONE SINGER ONE SONG

No joining in.

Say what you like about Neil Diamond, but he's on to something with that "Sweet Caroline." Because no matter whether you like him or not, no matter where you are, no matter whether you do actually know somebody called Caroline and she's a frickin' pain in the arse, it's impossible not to join in with the *bahbah bah baaa*.

Somebody got angry with me this week. Quite out of the blue. A woman I'd never met before suddenly let rip that she'd had enough, and my attitude was the cherry on the cake of her past few months.

I was quite surprised. I hadn't thought I had an attitude. She'd just stated that she believed things to be one way, and expected me to believe the same, and when I said I didn't agree, she blew a gasket.

In her defense, I do have one of those faces - when I'm not actually smiling, nature has blessed me with a face that looks like I'm mad about something. (It could be worse - when Mark isn't actually smiling, his face looks like he thinks you're a bloody idiot - or maybe that's just me.)

But in my defense, I wasn't mad at her, and I wasn't trying to prove a point. She just stated what she believed to be a universal truth, and I clarified that it wasn't universal. It wasn't anything personal.

Anyway, the point is, it obviously riled her. And she got pretty angry. So angry in fact, that I thought about joining in, and getting angry back at her.

It's a weird thing anger. It's totally like the song Sweet Caroline. Because even when you really don't want to, when you hear the cue, it's so hard not to *bahbah bah baaah*

But when I considered it, I could have maybe mustered a pissed-off attitude, or a defiant look of displeasure. I was mostly just a bit surprised and didn't know what I should be angry about other than she'd given me a bit of a fright. So I just sat there and let her let rip.

It wasn't long before what she was ranting about became not about me. It became about stuff that -I can't tell you in case she reads this - well, stuff that I'd be angry about too, and sad, and disappointed and hurt. And I was glad I hadn't said anything mean back to her. In the end she apologized, and I said it was fine and we went our separate ways. I don't expect I'm her favorite person, but then she isn't mine either.

Anyway, I was making breakfast yesterday, and Sweet Caroline came on Pandora and I willfully stopped myself *bahbah bah baaa-ing*. In fact, as I poured hot water onto a teabag I muttered to myself, "Fuck you,

Neil Diamond. You don't get to force-feed me your distorted manifesto of women called Caroline."

Though if I'm 100% honest, I may have unwittingly joined in on "Hands touching hands" while buttering my toast.

Still, say what you like about Neil Diamond, but I tell you he's on to something.

STARS AND STRIPES

10 years.

One December night when my eldest son was 10, we found his pet hamster still and lifeless, curled up in its little bed, looking to the world to be fast asleep. My son, glassy-eyed, asked me if he was going to be ok. Could I make him ok?

I said I didn't know, but we could try.

We sat by the fire trying to warm the hamster's little body but, after a while, it was clear (to me) that he was dead.

It was a Friday and Mark and I were going out and leaving the kids with a babysitter. I didn't want to go out. I wanted to stay home. I didn't want to make small talk with strangers. But I didn't want to talk about anything in the real world either. Mark and I were booked to go out for a Christmas party. We didn't want to go. Nobody wanted to go out. The news of a little elementary school in Connecticut and 26 families who would never see Christmas the same way again, hung in the air.

I said to my son that maybe "Stripes" was just hibernating, and that if we wrapped him in a warm blanket, maybe in the morning he might wake up. And I kissed my boys goodnight, and went out to a party, where other parents stood as we did. Making small talk just as we did. Studiously avoiding any discussion of the news as we did. Wearing our Christmas best, and our politest expressions, and doing anything to hide our feelings of horror and grief, and guilt, such enormous guilt, at our relief that it hadn't been our children's school.

In the morning my son climbed into my bed. Snuggling up, tearful, he said he didn't think Stripes had moved. I asked him if he wanted me to come and see.
He said he did, because he still had hope.

Then (because he's who he is) he explained how there will always be hope, because that's what Pandora managed to hold on to, when she opened the box and let evil into the world.

Later that day we had a funeral for Stripes. It was sad and sorry, but natural that their comprehension of death was one furry wee body snuggled in pet bedding and buried in the corner of the garden.

My eldest son is now 20. He has grown into a man. He used to want Transformers or Power Rangers or the latest computer game, but now he's happy when Santa brings him money in envelopes, and new trousers or shirts or socks or 'a surprise.'

And each December as I gather together Christmas gifts for my child who is no longer a child, I can't help but remember those who will never grow up, and my wounded rage is salted by thoughts and prayers, and thoughts and prayers, and thoughts and fucking prayers. Because if Sandy Hook wasn't enough to make the change, what is?

Soon. Sooner than it ever should. News will come...

An active shooter.

And I won't want them to go to school.
And I won't want there to be any schools anymore.
Because people can't be trusted. Because nobody can be trusted.
I'll want to stay home. I'll want us all to stay home. Safe. protected. Secure.
And I'll lie awake at night terrified of the world I've brought my sons into.

And then I'll take a breath, and then another. And I'll remind myself to be grateful. Because at least that bitch Pandora managed to hold on to something.

THE BEST THINGS...

..tend not to be two for a fiver.

I used to phone my Mum every Sunday. Now she's no longer here, I send a wee note out to you in the Universe instead. But at this time of year, she's on my mind a lot.

My mother liked a whole lot of things: Coronation street. Chocolate Gingers. Ricky Martin, and she really really liked a bargain.

One Christmas - when my sister and I were fully grown adults - she presented us both with "Christmas Robins" that she cheerfully announced she'd found on sale. "Aren't they lovely?"

The term 'lovely' was loose: Suppose your cat ate a cuddly toy, then vomited parts of it back up, and then someone gathered the parts and glued them together to make an animatronic toy bird on a perch - That level of lovely.

"They sing!" my Mum announced cheerfully- as if this could possibly be a good thing.

My sister, Janice, is open-minded about terrible Christmas ornaments: When I was about 10 I gave her, and my brother-in-law, what I thought, was a charming reindeer candle holder for their Christmas table. Oh how she had laughed. I thought it was because it was so adorable.

It wasn't till many years later when sitting at Janice's Christmas table that I noticed that the way the reindeer held the candle made it look like it had an enormous penis. (depending on the size of the candle.) And I understood why she'd laughed.

Anyway, even Janice who has a tolerance for dodgy Christmas ornaments, looked at the Robins doubtfully.

"They were two for a fiver. " My mum said, thrilled "Can you believe it?"

Janice and I did that thing where we made our faces smile.

"And, " she added - as if this was an added bonus - 'They're motion activated, so if you just walk past them, that's how they sing."

To prove a point, she switched on a robin and moved her hand over the sensor. It did indeed begin to 'sing'.

I use that term loosely: Suppose you had an old stylophone and your cat ate it, then vomited parts of it back up again, and miraculously it could still almost autoplay a couple of songs. - It was that level of 'singing'.

"My mother beamed," I know the kids will love them."

Fairly unsurprisingly, the kids did not love them. In fact, the first time my youngest heard one, he burst into tears.

Obviously, I considered throwing the robin out, but then decided against it. Around that time, that self-same kid used to get up in the middle of the night and steal cookies, and completely deny it the next day. Well, we both discovered one night, that there's nothing better than a motion-activated Christmas Robin to scare the absolute crap out of any unsuspecting, cookie thief. And so there was peace on earth - or at least around the cookie jar.

My ugly wee Christmas Robin has survived several house moves - one across a continent - and still lived to 'sing' the tale. And every year as the Christmas decorations are pulled out, out it comes too.

I'd like to say that over the years it has become more adorable, but I'd be lying. It's still a miniature version of entertainment hell resembling something a cat regurgitated.

I miss my mother for a million reasons. I probably always will. And that wee fake fur monstrosity never fails to remind me that the greatest gifts I've been given in life never came wrapped in Christmas paper.

So if you're heading into the holiday and feeling chipper, I send a big festive cheer and a Happy Christmas hoorah! And if you're heading into the holiday and you're struggling, I send a cuddle, and a virtual reindeer candelabra with a big penis, to remind you that one day you'll look back on now with very different eyes.

Dec 25, 2022

ARTHUR'S HOLIDAY THOUGHTS

Life is the gift. All that other stuff.... is just stuff.

Peace and love,

Lynn

x

Jan 1, 2023

IF YOU'RE HAPPY AND YOU KNOW IT... SHUT YOUR FACE

I do like names that can also be an instruction: Neil, Bob, Russell, Piers. Phil, Cary (and Grant - double whammy) Blanche, Chuck, Pat, and Chase. No surprise at all then, that I should marry a guy called Mark.

In life though, it's Mark who likes the actual instructions. You know when you buy a new thing, he's the guy who'll actually read the booklet of instructions that come with it. (I mean, who actually does that?)

I'm not so keen on names that can also be an adjective: Dusty, Lucky, Merry, Bonnie - though I'm pretty sure that's because of a tricky experience with a Happy.

My first child was born 5 weeks prematurely. The pregnancy had been a bit of a white knuckle ride, so after he was born we spent a week in hospital, me on a ward, and him in special care.

There's this very annoying thing about babies, in that when you have one, it's almost impossible to be calm when they're out of sight. I spent so much time sitting on the orange plastic chair next to my son's incubator, that the staff saw me as part of the furniture.

One night, there was a new face sitting opposite me. While Beth who worked night shift, pottered about with clipboards and quiet efficiency, a staff member I'd never seen before sat between two incubators on the other side of the room, holding a small baby. We'd nodded each other a hello when I'd arrived but nothing else.

There's a particular type of quiet in special care baby wards in the middle of the night: An occasional beep of a monitor, or the burr or machines, and the breathing of tiny lungs. That's why it felt strange that when Beth left for her break, the nurse sitting opposite me, decided she wanted to talk.

"I'm happy," she said.

"That's nice," I whispered.

I fussed with my son a little. Seeing him resting contentedly on my chest was such an intense mix of feelings. Life was everything. Everything. Once we made it through this part of the journey, I wouldn't let anything bother me again. I relaxed back on my plastic chair and closed my eyes.

"No, my name is Happy," said the woman more insistently.

I opened my eyes. Smiled a polite smile and closed them again.

Then I heard the scrape of a chair. I opened my eyes. With purpose, 'Happy' was walking towards me. I suddenly felt very awake.

She stood close to me. Looking down on my chair, she said, "Do you believe in the Lord Jesus Christ?"

"Oh well... ehm uh huh oh... mnn. " I smiled.

"Because I do." she continued, "I believe in the Lord Jesus." She leaned in close. "And through the Divine Power of Christ Almighty, these hands of mine heal all the little children."

In the pre-dawn light, we stared eye to eye. I wanted to say to her that I expected the Lord Jesus Christ might have words about scaring the crap out of new mothers in the middle of the night. Or maybe I could facetiously ask if the saving of the babies' lives was conditional on their parents' belief system. But the truth is, I said none of that. There was a certainty in her eye that worried me. I held onto my newborn son, acutely aware of my vulnerability.

"Oh well, Happy," I said, "That's really very good of you. I'm sure everybody is very grateful."

Happy stared at me. Calculating. My blood ran cold. There was a moment when I knew something was about to happen. I just couldn't work out what.

But then Beth appeared back from her break, bright and breezy. As if nothing had ever happened, and nothing at all had been said, Happy returned to her seat.

For the rest of the night, I sat in the orange plastic chair with my son clasped to my chest. My eyes were closed but my ears were on high alert, listening for any sign of movement from across the room.

The next day, I talked to the Chief of Staff about Happy and her divine healing powers. They agreed that medicine may also have had something to do with each baby's recovery, and that each parent's religious belief or lack of it wasn't appropriate discussion at 3 in the morning in a special care ward. The matter was dealt with.

My tiny little premature baby is now over 6 foot tall and faced with the 'divine healing hands' of any wide-eyed stranger in the middle of the night, would reach to protect me, rather than the other way round.

As we head into this new year, there's a precariousness in the air that is hard to ignore. These past few years have been rough and uncertain in the weirdest of ways. From time to time, I've found myself feeling a little bit like I did all those years ago in the pre-dawn light of a special care ward: Acutely aware of life's beauty and also its frailty. How much our own happiness is tethered in those we love. And my own infuriating powerlessness.

I thought about Happy recently when someone wished me Happy New Year. And I laughed. And thought no thanks. I don't fancy seeing her again in any new year.

But then I had a wee change of perspective. Because what that oddly named woman showed me all those years ago, was that things that frickin terrify you in the middle of the night, tend to work out just fine in the light of day. The truth about life is that brilliant stuff happens all the time. It's just that crazy is better at attracting attention.

And with that, I wish you a Happy New Year. May the things that currently worry you, be nothing more than interesting stories in the not-too-distant future.

Jan 8, 2023

WORLD DOMINATION POSTPONED

Soup recipes welcome

I don't know when it all changed, but I do know that when I was a kid, people were content with being teachers, policemen, firemen, or post office workers. A couple of my parents' friends were actually almost cocky about being accountants.

I remember the neighbors loudly boasting about the exotic prospects of their son studying to become a metallurgist, and a couple of my Mum's friends bringing round a cake to celebrate the fact that their daughter had just been promoted to a management position in the local McDonald's.

But it seems those days are gone. Now it's not enough to work. Now, you have to have a purpose as well.

Unless an accountant is simultaneously conquering Everest in their spare time, they are described as 'just an accountant." No prospective Metallurgist is exciting unless they have a YouTube channel, an Instagram account, a couple of TED talks, a sexy ass, and a thrilling TikTok channel. And if someone were to say their kid worked at McDonalds, the following question would be, "And what are they really up to the rest of the time?"

I understand the way social media works and that people are meant to tell you their good things, but if early humans had behaved in the way we're all supposed to now, cave drawings would have everybody doing jazz hands.

So do we really all have to be 'special'? Because, the fact is, when I look at people who are supposedly special, I can't honestly muster any excitement for it.

I'm reluctant to mention the name Elon Musk - because it's like feeding the giant attention monster - but possibly the only thing his supposed genius has taught me, is that having all the money and power in the world definitely doesn't make you a happy person. If it did, he wouldn't be so bloody whiny all the time.

Now you may be sensing I have a bit of 'an attitude'. And you'd be completely right. I am defiant because it's been raining in the Valley this week and I can't really be arsed doing anything apart from pottering about in a cozy jersey and maybe making a pot of soup. And I feel guilty about it. But then I think why? Who am I harming by doing buggar all? When did the activity of just pottering about being contented in your own skin become a luxury to be kept for holidays or special occasions?

I'm all for self-improvement and all that, but there are times when it's good to say, I'm doing the best that I can right now. And considering the ups and downs and general weirdness of 2022, we should each be getting a merit badge for coming through it.

If you ask me - you didn't, but I'm telling you anyway, because like I said, it's been raining in LA and I'm feeling defiant - world domination can wait. Today in the comfort of some flannelette-based clothing, I can proudly announce I will be doing nothing of historical importance. I victoriously declare myself spectacularly unspectacular. Though if I'm honest, I may be making a mighty tasty pot of soup.

Jan 15, 2023

TICKLING STICK

I've been a bit of a weather-obsessed of late but, in my
defense, there has been actual real weather in The
Valley this past few weeks and it's unusual. Normally we
just have: Hot. Frickin' hot. Really frickin' hot. Fuckit
you're on fire and 'Gee it's a bit misty'. But this week,
there's not only been rain, but actual thunder and
lightning as well.

It's messed up a lot of California, but there hasn't -
thankfully - been too much of an effect round here in
Tweddley Manor.

My kids don't care about the weather unless it affects
their Wi-Fi signal. Mark is fine unless the trees are
dropping branches on his car. Even the chickens don't
seem to mind it much and are out looking for snacks,
rain or shine. Admittedly Genghis the rooster prefers to
stay in the coop though that's less that he's anxious, as
much as the damp-feathered look cramps his
Casanova-esque style.

Struggling with it most is Arthur. Turns out dogs don't
like walking or pooping in the rain. And the thunder
absolutely terrifies him. Even thunder that's too far away
for me to hear, gives him the shakes.

Watching him, I wonder why, when he's so evidently
safe and warm, it bothers him so much. Is it because it's
an unusual sound or because of an actual experience?

By that I mean, is his fear instinctive or has it been learned?

You see, I have an on-and-off fear of money. I have a tendency to think of it like a lion that can't be tamed - one I have to be very careful around it, or it will bite me in the ass. Yet the grown-up part of me knows that money is just an object, like a plate or a shoe or an apple, and it's my relationship towards it that gives it its power. But my parents struggled with the unpredictability of money when I was small, so even though I do my best to persuade myself otherwise, it seems only reasonable that I should struggle too.

Annoyingly, the things we inherit are not always the things we'd choose.

My mother struggled her whole life thinking she was fat, just as her own mother had. And truly, both of them always looked pretty beautiful to me.

When our kids were wee, I told them thunder was caused by the clouds tickling each other and the roaring noise was them laughing. Lightning, I explained, was that the clouds were being tickled too much, and laughing so hard they might be sick. That's why when there's lightning, it's better to stay out of the way - because everyone knows that when there's tickling going on, you might get hit by a rogue arm or leg. As a result, my kids view thunder the same way they view their parents cuddling in the kitchen - 'unpleasant but harmless,' and shrug it off and get on with their lives.

I like that. In fact, I like it so much, I may steal it back. (Who says you only get to inherit attitudes from your parents?) I bet there are plenty of times I could apply the 'unpleasant but harmless' rule to things that hit me by surprise. Stuff happens I may not love, but that doesn't have to make me scared. Thunder isn't personal after all, and worrying and fear have never brought me anything apart from sleepless nights.

I explained as much to Arthur when he was trembling from the noise of the storm. I said, "Arthur, you know that's just the sound of the clouds laughing." And for a moment, he actually stopped shaking - just long enough to look at me like I'm a complete frickin' idiot. Then he started shaking again.

So I offered him a snack - and that seemed to help.

KNOW YOUR LINES

We have one of those pink 40s bathrooms, which I love and hate at the same time. Though the tiles are beautiful, they're a weird shade of salmon pink that, in certain lights, can feel like you're living inside some 70s soft-porn telemovie set. And that, my friends, is not a place where you feel like brushing your teeth of a morning.

So I decided I was going to paint the walls. I don't care that there are a million other things I could/ should be doing. Change is good.

When I told Mark my idea for the new decor he looked doubtful. Then he asked if I had been *Yabba Dabba Dooed*.

I should explain.

There are many notable landmarks in our area - by that I mean they're notable to Mark and me and probably nobody else - as they're on the path of our regular dog walk.

There's "Dog Poo Alley" - an unpaved shortcut between two houses where people - some of them irresponsible - walk their dogs. (Wandering through there in flip-flops is the local equivalent of Russian Roulette.)

Then there's The Important People's Residence - so called because the inhabitants always seem to be very very busy and heading somewhere to do something very very important. There's the Breaking Bad house - something dodgy is going on in there. (Honestly who needs to black out all their windows?)

But my absolute favorite of them all is Yabba Dabba Doo corner, so called because the fence round the yard there is more than a little Flintstoney.

Now I don't know the people who live there. I've never met them, yet I feel they are my spirit animals. Because in an area that is increasingly smart wooden picket fences or trimmed hedges or expensive ironwork, these guys blatantly do not give a fuck. Not only have they erected a fence that looks like the kind of stonework you'd find around a castle, over Christmas, they decided no Christmas light was too much - or too weird. They have freely and resolutely given up sophistication for happiness. And I am their fan.

So when Mark asked if I'd been *Yabba Dabba Dooed*, he meant had I allowed my fandom to take over.

I explained to him (patiently, I thought) that the world has felt so bleak of late -I mean, jeez, January has been very Januaryish - and I want to push against it with a bit of cheery.

"There's so much I can't change, and I can dwell on that and allow it to piss me off. Or I can at least decide not to brush my teeth in a 70s porn set." I said.

Mark remained unconvinced. So then I told him that it was only paint and if it turned out too mental, I could paint over it. He nodded, muttered something, and headed off to his office and I called after him that it really wasn't that extreme.

And it wasn't. I just wanted to do stripes. Big ones. Vertical. Black and white. That's all.

Anyway, it took a bit of work and a couple of dozen rolls of masking tape, but it's done, and I like it.

Mark says he's glad I'm happy, though he does feel it's like peeing in a circus.

"And that's a marvelous thing, right?" I said.

Again, he muttered something and headed off to his office.

One day maybe I'll invite all the neighbors round - apart from the Breaking Bad ones - and the Important People who'd be too busy to come anyway. And some of them may worry that I've lost my frickin' mind. And they may well indeed be right. But the Yabba Dabba Doo neighbors will nod their approval - knowingly - and I will be completely thrilled.

[For photos of the bathroom stripes: https://www.lynnfergy.com/p/know-your-lines]

WHEN THE BEE STINGS

Dulcius Ex Asperis

My Dad didn't speak much Latin. Fairly unsurprisingly, being able to talk like an ancient Roman isn't high on the list of priorities for people working for the post office in Scotland. But that did not stop him from periodically proclaiming, "Dulcius Ex Asperis"

For all you non Latin speakers, it means 'Sweeter After Difficulty.' It's the Ferguson motto on the Clan crest, which is a bee on a jaggy thistle. (Maybe because Fergusons throughout history have a fair amount of jagged edges.)

My Dad wasn't a man who talked a lot, but he had a few phrases he was fond of that he utilized when he thought fit, such as "Never trust a man who dyes his hair," or "Put your money in the box" - which he loved to say when he answered the phone. But his favorite of all was 'sweeter after difficulty.'

Difficulty is part of the nature of things. Like the flow of the tides. When it comes, it can hurt, damage, destroy. It can knock you sideways, but it can't ever break you, not without your say-so.
And like the tides, difficulty will pass. It has to. And nothing feels sweeter than getting back on your feet

again. Stretching your arms out and taking a breath. Strong.

My Dad liked to wear check shirts. (long-sleeved in Winter, short-sleeved in Summer) He wore socks and sandals when wearing shorts. He had the bluest of blue eyes, and his nose would take on gigantic bulbous proportions with too much sun.

He and my mum met at the dancing when they were young. Before my Mum's arthritis, they used to enjoy a dance. He was nimble on his feet.

He loved when Shirley Bassey was on TV, and would suck the air through his teeth whenever there were snakes. He had the most hilarious arguments with my Mum about how to cook fish.

Even though he was born and bred in Glasgow, he's still the undisputed inventor of "Chinese Egg" which looks and tastes exactly like hot boiled eggs, butter, toast, and salt mixed together in a cup - but is obviously much much more exotic.

17 years ago this week I looked down at his body on a hospital bed, trying to comprehend how he could be gone forever. It was impossible. Wrong. So wrong. Even though I know it is the Nature of things.

Yet still I see him in my own hands, in my youngest son's unruly hair, in my elder son's bluest of blue eyes.

Sweeter.

In my mind, my Mum and Dad are on a cruise in the Bahamas. The ship has all the mod cons apart from (ridiculously) phone reception and WIFI, so they can't get in touch. My parents really should complain about that, but they're having such a good time they don't.

My Dad is wearing shorts, a short-sleeved check shirt, and socks and sandals. His nose has taken on gigantic bulbous proportions because of too much sun. He and my Mum have been upgraded to the very best suite - on account of the Head Chef being humbled to have the creator of Chinese Egg on board.

In the evenings they dress up. They sit at the Captain's table, or are nimble on the dance floor. Far away from snakes. To the music of Shirley Bassey.

Sweeter.

But every year on this week, the tide comes in. It's inevitable.

Every year at this time, I'm reminded who I am.

Feb 5, 2023

LESS OF THE PROVERBS, MORE OF THE FOOTCARE.

The proverb, "Familiarity breeds contempt," was clearly invented by an idiot.

And, the fact that I can so contemptuously make that statement about some proverb-making stranger only goes to prove my point.

Some claim the original writer was Chaucer. Others claim it was Aesop. But nobody really knows, which again completely proves my point. Because, if the Proverb-Making Stranger had more familiarity in his/her life, they'd have had someone bothering to record that detail for prosperity.

I am pro-familiarity. It gives a sense of belonging, of inclusion, of a weird kind of safety. Like when Mark and I are out walking Arthur, we generally bump into people from the area - some we're friendly with, and others we're only on polite smiling with - and I like that. It feels like community.

I'm not talking over-familiarity obviously. That's a whole different issue. (I am still Scottish after all.) If our Proverb-Making Stranger had proclaimed "Over familiarity breeds the likelihood of a punch in the face," I'd have no complaints.

And contempt is a very strong word. Yet I admit, I'm not a stranger to it.

Periodically, a grey-colored cat comes into our backyard and frightens the chickens. Just for fun. When I see that cat I am full of contempt. But that's not because it's familiar to me. It's because that cat is a straight-up douchebag, and everybody in the neighborhood knows it. (sorry, cat lovers)

Familiarity is something completely different.

I have a pair of black, leather, ankle boots I've owned for more years than I care to remember. I bought them in a shop that no longer exists on Oxford St, London. They were mine before I was married, before I became a Mum, before I moved to the Valley, and before I'd even thought about living in the US. These boots have been in my life since before I had any sense of the three people I live with now.

Originally I bought them for stand-up - which requires practical footwear: You want to be able to get on a stage easily, and get off with incredible speed (trust me) if need be. But over the years they've evolved to every sort of event footwear. They're what I wear when "I'm not sure what to expect, so best be adaptable."

They've been re-heeled a couple of times and are always in need of a polish, but when I open the closet and see them, I get that warm cozy feeling that comes from something familiar.

They're stored alongside several pairs of high heels that are still in boxes. These shoes are a lot fancier and cost much more than the boots, yet I've barely worn them because they're so bloody uncomfortable.

Every time my eye catches the boxes, I think about how I should get rid of them. But I paid so much for them that I figure I should keep them until they pay for themselves.

But they're so bloody uncomfortable, I'm never going to wear them. So they're never going to pay for themselves.

(And what does that even mean anyway? Like what are they going to do? Get a part-time job?)

Every time I see those shoe boxes, I contemptuously mutter 'What the Hell was I thinking?"

But truthfully, I can tell you what I was thinking. I was thinking, "Oooh I can't wear old stuff to a fancy occasion. I need something new and swanky." It wasn't that I was seeing my familiar stuff with contempt. But stupidly, I was worried some random stranger might.

One day during the Pandemic when I opened my closet, I thought about how the value of shoes had completely changed: What's the point of any of them at all if you have nowhere to go? And even then if you are going somewhere, shouldn't you be comfortable enough to experience it?

Who cares what something looks like, it's what it feels like that's the key. In life, you can't always know what to expect, so it's best to be adaptable.

You know, I'm not averse to the old proverb or two, but frankly if Aesop or Chaucer or the Proverb-Making-Stranger had thought they needed to wear high heels to look important, the whole proverb-making world would have been completely different.

For a start, there'd be more along the lines of, "Familiarity breeds content."

PROPER VALENTINE'S BULLSHIT.

A couple of years ago Mark bought me 12 bags of Steer Manure (bullshit) for Valentine's Day, and I couldn't have been happier.

I'd had dreams of planting a hedgerow in the backyard, so we couldn't see into the neighbors. It's quite a big space though, so the budget only allowed for small hedge plants.

 Yet there is no greater love than a wee hedge plant has for steer manure. It is a horticultural Dr Zhivago, and now my hedgerow dream is a reality.

I used to dread this week as a teenager. I didn't want cards, but I did. And the boys I wanted to send me cards were never card-sending type. And the boys who would have sent me a card, were definitely not my type. Waking up on Valentine's morning to a card -blatantly sent from my Mum - I'd feel I was a failure.

Now, as someone whose been married for more than 20 years, I tend to view Valentine's day as a bit of a pain in the arse. One of the greatest gifts in finding who you want to live your life with, is that you get to tell them you love them any time you want.

As I see the heart-shaped cards appearing in the stores, almost the day after Christmas, I've grown to suspect

Valentine's Day is primarily made to boost the profits of cheesy card makers, and to antagonize single people.

Here in the US kids are encouraged to send everybody in their class a Valentine. I like that. Everybody has a right to feel they matter.

And real love isn't all hearts and flowers. Sometimes it's frankly brutal.

My eldest had a convulsion when he was three years old. I still remember watching the body of this tiny little human and thinking I would give my life for him, right there and then, if only he could be ok again.

I know that's love. But I doubt you'll find it written in rhyming form on the inside of a card of a cat playing a banjo.

I'd like to put it out there that love isn't stationary dependent. Sometimes those we really love can't show us they love us back. Sometimes because they're not capable. Sometimes they don't want to. Sometimes because they're no longer here. (I would love to wake up to one of those Valentine cards blatantly from my Mum now, but that's not going to happen.)

If Valentine's Day is obligatory, I would wish for it to celebrate the existence of love. It could be a reminder that in an increasingly difficult world, love exists not just in heart shapes, but in all different shapes. Maybe it's a bit like pollen. It's in the air. Sometimes you're really affected by it. Sometimes you barely notice it at all. But without it, we'd not last long.

Big fat beautiful love. Dolloped right in the middle of all that is. Hidden amongst yearning and sorrow and fear. Bold and brilliant. Hanging out with its best pal, Hope.

Starting Notes From The Valley was about love. I used to call my Mum every Sunday. Now she's gone, I send a note out into the Universe instead.

In reading the note, you connect back - some of you mad, crazy kids even listen to my recordings - and for me, there is healing. I'm not suggesting we all set up house any time soon, but it's like a tiny bit of pollen.

So consider this my Valentine, wherever you may be. In gratitude for you being you, I am sending you a virtual version of the best Valentine's present I ever received -12 bags of Prime Steer Manure.

May whatever dream you want to plant, grow magnificently.

PEOPLE VERSUS PEACHES

Trust your gut

My youngest son has always been solid. From the moment he opened his tiny eyes on the world and decided it was satisfactory, he was clear about what works for him.

When we decided it was time for him to stop using pacifiers (dummies in the UK) because he had teeth growing in, he found a way to stash them in different places around the house. So when we thought we reclaimed them all, he'd toddle into the room, chewing victoriously on a pacifier like a gangster with a cigar.

He didn't bother speaking until he could master full sentences. If anyone tried baby language on him, he'd look at them like they were deranged. He's always been his own person, preferring to hang out in small groups and well away from drama.

So it was a surprise when his preschool called to say that he'd caused a fracas during 'fruit time."

Apparently, he had refused to eat fruit and wouldn't be reasoned with. His uncompromising rebellion had brought on a full Spartacus moment, with an entire classroom of 3-year-olds refusing their fruit too. So he'd been sent to the Principal's office to explain himself, and so the other kids would calm down.

He sat on the time-out chair, his head down, swinging his chubby little legs, forlornly. When the Principal asked him if he knew why he was there, he nodded. He looked her straight in the eye and stated with great gravitas, "I don't like peaches."

Trying not to laugh, she asked why he'd been shouting. He said he'd told Miss Betsy he didn't like peaches but she kept telling him he did, and she wouldn't listen so he had to shout. He agreed he'd say sorry for disrupting "fwoot time" but he'd only promise not to do it again, if they promised they wouldn't try to make him eat peaches.

His 'no peanuts' rule came into place, somewhere around the beginning of elementary school. He came home outraged one day, as he'd been put at a lunch table where people were openly eating peanuts. He insisted I tell the teacher that he absolutely had to be on the 'No Peanuts' table, because his life was in danger.

I didn't think he was allergic to peanuts, though we aren't a particularly peanut family, so it hadn't crossed my mind. But he was pretty adamant about the 'danger'. So we talked to the teacher, and he was moved to the 'No Peanuts" table, and all was good.

A couple of years later, shortly after Valentine's Day, we were pottering about the house and suddenly he started screaming. He ran out of his room, his skin purple, vomiting and choking, his eyes wide with panic. "Poison! Poison!" he gasped.

I took him to the bathroom and held his head while his little body tried to expel whatever was in there. Mark went to see what he had eaten, and found the wrapper for a peanut butter cup that had been stashed away with Valentine candy he got from friends.

We gave him water and some antihistamine, and fairly quickly he was fine. Tired, emotional, but fine. So, we took him to get allergy tested. Turns out he is VERY allergic to peanuts. He even got his own epi-pen.

He knew. Before we knew. Before there was any reason for anybody to know, he knew. And he trusted his gut.

The peanut episode was a big lesson for Mark and I. In fact, maybe one of these days, I'll write my parenting book: "Before Giving Birth To You, I'd No Idea About Any Of This Stuff, So I'm Winging It," because I've learned so much from my kids.

If either one of the boys tells us something is true, we start by believing them - no matter how unpleasant or implausible it might be. That alone has proved to be completely bloody invaluable over the years.

That wasn't necessarily the way things worked when we were kids: "Tough shit if you don't like peaches." "You don't talk back to adults." "A food allergy is just showing off." Maybe I should dedicate a chapter to it in my parenting book, called "They Were Winging It Too."

The world I grew up in seems very different from the one my kids are growing up in now. And I can't help feeling I had it so much easier.

Another school shooting in the US this week and the only thing that surprises me is how numb I've become. I'm cooking dinner when my 15-year-old comes in for a cuddle, because he's upset. I hug him and ask him what's wrong. He tells me he's scared. He says he and his friends have been discussing the school's active shooter drill and they don't think they'd have much of a chance of escape. He says they're worried that there's a store selling guns about a mile away.

I tell him he'll be ok. I tell him about California's gun laws. I throw in some statistics that might be helpful, like how it's more dangerous crossing a road.

I remind him how good he is at hide and seek. I point out how his father would walk through fire for him, if only just to bore him with TikTok videos he's found.

He smiles. And we're ok. We both agree we're ok.

And we have dinner and move on, because there is no chapter in any parenting book for this.

I am glad my son is solid. I am fine that he doesn't like peaches. I am thrilled he is able to say no to those in authority who tell him he has to accept what is unacceptable. That gives me hope for the future. Because what is happening is fucking unacceptable

But right now, when he goes to school and I feel the tightness in my stomach, I remind myself that he, above all people, knows how to listen to his gut when it tells him something is dangerous. And I am grateful.

BEST LEAVE IT TO GWYNETH

Cold paddling

It's been windy round these parts this week - and I don't mean in a digestive way. California has had a proper bout of weather: rain and wind, and more rain and a bit more wind, and thunder, lightning, and flooding. It's been tricky for people because of power outages due to fallen trees. Here at Tweddley Manor, we've been OK so far, and even though we're surrounded by a lot of trees, weirdly I've found the sound of the wind in them strangely reassuring.

Scotland is a place that gets a lot of weather - sometimes all 4 seasons in one day. I remember on one particularly blustery Winter's day when I was a teenager, my Mum looking out of the window and asking, "Do you think the trees panic when they lose all their leaves in the Winter and worry it might never be Spring again?"

I'd love to know what was going on in her head at the time. My Mum talked about a lot of things. She would talk about worry in terms of, "I'm worried about you going out without a jacket on," but not other worries. Not the worries I know now as an adult we all have.

But I do know that life is bumpy. And when it is, your mind can go to all sorts of places.

Around 25 years ago, I was walking on Holkham beach in the UK. The very same beach where Gwyneth Paltrow walked for that scene in Shakespeare in Love - and there all similarity with me and Gwyneth probably ends, apart from that we're both female and bi-peds.

When the tide is high in Holkham it looks pretty much like any other picturesque coastal area. But when the tide goes out, the sea almost disappears. The beach stretches for miles and miles. In fact, the sea goes so far out, it's hard to believe there'd ever been water there.

I walked alone. I had thinking to do. I knew I had to end a relationship. It wasn't good and hadn't been for a while. But I had so much invested in it, I almost didn't know me without the other person. So I didn't know that I could. Truthfully, I was scared.

But once you know something you can't unknow it. You can pretend, or tell yourself you'll handle it later, or it will get better. But it never gets better. It only gets darker.

I've never been like one of those smiling "Feel like a change?" hair dye adverts. When I make a change it's because there is no alternative. So I was trying to find an alternative.

Walking along this vast plateau of sand towards the water, I wondered if anyone ever panicked that the sea wouldn't come in again. That it had gone forever. Nobody seemed to. Everyone around seemed to be having a lovely time. Down at the shoreline, there was a couple of kids playing with a ball. A little further along there was a guy walking a dog. Behind me, two women rode horses along the sand. Sea birds cawed overhead in a blue sky filled with puffy white clouds.

When I finally reached the shoreline, I rolled up my jeans and stood with my feet in the water, looking as unlike Gwyneth Paltrow as it is possible to look. The water was cold, but good.

Wiggling my toes, I laughed to myself about how I'd just asked myself my own version of my mother's about the trees. Why would anyone panic about the tide not returning, when they knew from experience that the moon would make it so? Why would the trees panic about losing their leaves when they know they have to shed to make room for the new? Why was I so afraid of change, when I know it's the core of the ebb and flow of life?

The place where my feet were was usually underwater. All around the beach, there were signs saying to be mindful of the tides. Pretty soon the tide would come in. There's danger in not adapting to what is. No point in ignoring the signs.

I turned and walked back towards the land. I knew what needed to be done and knew I'd be OK. Life would be different, but at some point along the line, I'd be OK.

Social media is both a blessing and a curse. It's wonderful to still be connected to people from years back, and still in some limited way journeying together. But everything is all about ebb and flow, and it's so tough to hear when people you care about are struggling.

I want to say to them, what my mother said to me all those years ago when, as a teenager, I faced a challenge I really thought might floor me. "Do you think trees panic when they lose their leaves in the Winter because they think it will never be Spring again?"

But I don't, because they'd probably think I was mental. And anyway, you have to be someone like Gwyneth Paltrow to get away with that kind of stuff.

WHAT CAME FIRST - THE CHICKEN, THE EGG, OR THE BAG OF CONCRETE?

Feathery wisdom

My eldest, Fergus, and I are pretty good pals. I like his company. He makes me laugh. He's not afraid to challenge me, and obviously sometimes I drive him crazy. Though, if we're honest, what's the point in actually having kids if you don't get to annoy them?

When he's around the house he helps me with the chickens and he proofreads my blog - so if there are typos and spelling mistakes in anything you've read so far, it's completely his fault.

Earlier this week as we were off collecting eggs, he mentioned that of late he's found my blog 'overly inspirational'.

"One Marianne Williamson is enough. Nobody needs another one. Especially not a Scottish one."

"Ooh," I said, "Am I writing too many memes?"

He cringed disgustedly, because I pronounced the word meme MEHM as opposed to MEEM which is how the kids all say it, apparently. I did it intentionally. I always do it intentionally. It's very satisfying. My kids find it almost as disturbing as when I used to try to do the floss dance.

"I am just saying maybe you could try writing something that didn't have a point to it," he said.

I replied that I'd spent a great deal of my career writing things with no particular point to them, to which he said - rather sarcastically I thought - that that would be impossible because I'm always so 'teachy'.

I would have responded with something witty and wise and totally "un-teachy" but when I opened the nesting box, Bruiser was in one of them sitting on a bunch of eggs. Unimpressed at being disturbed, she let out a less-than-charming squawk.

Bruiser's the eldest of our chickens. She got her name because she hatched first and had a tendency to plunge forward into situations without much thought. Now she's fully grown, she spends so much time trying to hatch random eggs, we should have called her Brooder.

"God's sake, Bruiser, not again. Can't you just wander about being a chicken instead of always having to prove something? "

Looking across at Fergus, I noticed he was smiling very smugly. And that is how we agreed that I would write this week's blog about chickens and it wouldn't be in the least bit 'inspirational'.

So, here we go:

We have 10 chickens - well, 9 and a rooster. We hatched most of them from eggs during a particularly bleak part of the pandemic when we wished to remind ourselves that amidst the bleakest of times, there's always birth. (apologies - I forgot myself)

I never expected them to have personalities. I thought they'd just be...well...chickens but they really are individuals. (I could say here something about how all living creatures have different perspectives and that's what makes up life's giant tapestry - but I won't because I'm a rule follower.)

Norma for example - the wee ginger chicken - is always up for some drama. Whenever there's a tussle, she's somewhere in the middle of it providing a running commentary. She's never knowingly laid an egg without announcing her achievements to the whole neighborhood. It's hard not to admire her feathery enthusiasm. She's like a wee bundle of feathery PR.

However, seeing the whole world only as an extension of herself, she kept pecking the other chickens' eggs. There comes a point in life when you have to lay down boundaries. (That's not inspirational, by the way. That's just a fact) In the end, we had to put a concrete egg in the coup. She pecked it once and the problem stopped.

On the downside, another problem began. The concrete egg attracted the attention of Bruiser, who appears to see it as a challenge.

Margaret, Senga, and Peggy are beautiful snow-white birds who go everywhere in a team. They stick together like glue. What one of them does, they all do. It's hard to tell them apart - especially from a distance - so we generally refer to them as 'the white trash.'

Nuggets and Poggers are like mad professors. They lay blue-green eggs and keep their distance. Nuggets is the chicken who most enjoys a cuddle, though she probably wouldn't if she knew the meaning of her name.

Then, there's Margo, the surreptitious chicken. She fits in everywhere but not with anyone in particular. She moves from group to group with ease. If Margo wasn't a chicken, she'd make a great spy.

Genghis is our rooster. I've heard talk about crazy aggressive roosters attacking people. Genghis likes to be hand-fed spaghetti, though he'd fight to the death to save his girls. He's followed by Shelley all the time. She's a veritable egg-laying Uriah Heep.

And then, of course, there's Bruiser.

"The thing is," I said to Ferg as we went out to get eggs yesterday, "When you don't have a point to a story, it's just a list. And when anybody talks about their lives there's always a point because we all live different lives. If my stuff sounds 'teachy' it's because I'm talking about what it is to be me and nobody knows more about what that is, than me."

Ferg eyed me calmly, "Have you had your first cup of tea yet?" he asked.

"No. Why?"

He nodded and smiled. "No reason."

"Look, I am just saying that in life, people are doing and saying meaningful things all the time. They just don't write them down. So they don't notice. If people were to write down every Sunday what happened to them that week, you can bet it would be inspirational."

Ferg picked up the egg box and went to open the coop.

"And a meme is just a moment in that. It's one single thought one person had as a response to something real. If you take any one single thought and lay it out in text over a photograph, that makes it profound. But it was inspirational all on its own to start with."

Fergus opened the nesting box. Bruiser squawked furiously and, surprised, he jumped.

"Goddammit, Bruiser! " he said. "You know, there is a difference between optimism and trying to hatch a concrete egg!"

As soon as it was out his mouth, he knew what he'd done. He looked at me. I returned his look, very smugly.

"That would look so lovely over a nice picture of an egg amongst some hay," I said.

And that is how we agreed on the picture for this week's blog.

There's a difference between optimism...

...and trying to hatch a concrete egg.

LynnFergy.com

HAND MODELING FOR THE OVER FIFTIES

Sprachen Sie Deutsch?

The weird thing about getting older is that you become less visible. Even though you've lived longer and seen more, somehow you become less relevant.

Mark and I are in the process of swanking up our wee guesthouse to rent out. We were out hunter-gathering this week and passed a youngish guy who was out in his front yard planting vegetables. We're not strangers to the growing of vegetables ourselves, so we stopped to compliment him on his beds and chat about the management of horticultural pests, but it was not to be.

Once the compliment about the growing conditions was over, he patronizingly yeah yeah yeahed us in the way my kids used to do when I asked if they'd done their homework. When I talked about my tomato seedlings, he literally looked at me as if I'd just boasted about my age while standing in the queue at the post office.

The fact is, he couldn't be arsed talking to us because we're old.

It crossed my mind that I could have said to him, "Look you wee hipster douchebag, I have shoes older than you, so how about sticking that patronizing attitude up your arse." But I didn't, obviously, because I'm lovely.

It's not a surprise to me that I've moved into an older demographic, it was just weird to be up close and personal to it. Hipster douchebag was no spring chick himself. I reckoned he was about 29 which is just about exactly the same age I feel I am inside.

When I was 29, I behaved a bit differently. I was up to a lot of mischief with my friend Ashley. We were such a dangerous combination. We were different but the same. She worked in the music business. I know buggar all about music - when she played me a pre-released early recording of the Spice Girls, I said I didn't see how they'd be famous. We'd go out drinking and say we were hand models and do different hand poses for people that we professed to be very "of the moment." Or we'd profess to work in the posh frock department of a very well-known upmarket London department store and advise people on their clothing for special occasions. My partner in crime, she showed up with a ticket to visit Graceland when my life was tricky. I was on a vacation with her when I discovered I'm fluent in German, but only when I drink rum.

Of course, time and life move on. 2 years ago I called her on her birthday. We laughed about stupid stuff. She told me loved me and that I was a nightmare, and I said I'd have a drink later and talk some German in her honor. She was dead two weeks later.

Friends are not supposed to die. We're not biologically programmed for that. I miss her. I will always miss her.

And the hipster douchebag with the wispy beard will never know her, and that will be his loss.

So I am perfectly aware that I am lucky that I get to get older, and also unlucky because it has to be without her.

Aging is inevitable. It's a gift. Admittedly it can be scary because of the physical stuff, but the truth is the physical stuff can get you at any time.

Why are we meant to be ashamed that we get old, especially since the very best thing about getting older is the lack of vanity?

Back when I was 29 Chesney Hawkes was a guy I knew from Top Of The Pops. Now we do a podcast together, his kids are friends with my kids, and Mark and I are friends with him and his wife Krissy.

When he goes off to the UK for work, he brings me back my 'old lady cream' that they sell over there. I did say to him once that I was worried he'd be spotted by some tabloid and there'd be the headline: "Chesney Hawkes uses old lady cream!" to which he replied, "Fuck it. I've been accused of much worse."

As we headed off from the hipster guy, I asked Mark if he'd noticed how the guy had blanked us because we were old.

"Who cares?", he said, "You have shoes older than him."

"Right!?!" I said. " I do. Want to hear about my tomato seedlings?"

"Oh go on then," he smiled.

I took his arm. "Alright, but let's go and buy me some Mai Tai, first. I'm thinking of speaking some German tonight."

POTPOURRI SHAMED

Oooh, what's that smell?

I don't know if you've been around long enough to know what potpourri is. Basically it's a mix of dried, sweet-smelling plants and stuff thrown in a pretty bowl to make your house smell nice. It was all over 'tasteful homes' in the 1990s.

Mark told me about a friend of his who was meeting his girlfriend's parents for the first time at a cocktail party. He was nervous and wanted to make the best impression. Suited and booted he turned up on his best behavior. Everything was going well until - the very pinnacle of sophistication - he reached into a bowl of potpourri thinking it was some form of fancy nut snack.

When he realized his mistake, he carried on crunching the twigs in his mouth until he could swallow, like there was nothing at all unusual. He knew he had to front it out, because if he showed shame he was done for. And, in his audacity, he went so far as to advise another guest to "stay away from those nuts as they're a bit bitter."

As a result, the parents found him, 'interesting'.

It's been a quiet week here at Tweddley Manor as I've been down with some cold/flu combo. Though I am full of gratitude for a warm safe place to have the lurgy in, the truth is I am a terrible patient.

I like to get stuff done. I am - as they say- a doing person. It's a pain in the arse. For me and for everybody. So I just kept going even though my brain felt fried and my body like it had taken a good kicking.

I finally sat down when Mark and the kids pointed out that my 'resilience' was just making everyone uncomfortable. I was unceremoniously plonked in front of the TV with a blanket and a hot drink and instructions to stay there until I properly felt better.

And that is how I decided to watch "The Vow" on HBO. It's about a cult called NXIVM. I have friends who wandered in and out of a cult by mistake, so I thought I'd take a peek.

It was an intense watch. The people who got caught up with their sociopathic leader, were smart, gentle, talented individuals with one fatal flaw: Their desire to do good was matched by a capacity to feel shame.

I am very suspicious of shame. I know it's a human emotion and therefore has its place, but it's never evenly distributed. Too many good people are crippled by a perceived shame, and too many who could be doing with a good old dollop of shame seem to be the least able to feel it.

Personally I prefer regret. Regret is more of a wee reminder to do things differently next time. Whereas shame is too much like, if you ever once peed your pants, you'll never ever be allowed to change your trousers.

There's no redemption. And come on, who doesn't love a good redemption?

Watching episode after episode - when not shouting, "Don't listen to him, he's a liar. In fact, he's a creepy liar" at the TV, - I'd be shaking my head sympathetically. You only have to have one awful teacher to recognize that shame is the twin of control. Surprisingly I found myself almost thankful for those lessons from Mrs Dunbar - who is currently burning in Hell.

When you make individuals ashamed of themselves - especially of things they have very little control over - you can have almost complete authority over them. It's like a magician's trick : distract someone by the severity of their inadequacies, and they'll be so preoccupied by their own failures, they'll barely notice any faults in their accuser

I drank more tea and took some more medicine, and sat in front of the TV. As time passed, I physically started to feel better, Though by the end of the last episode of "The Vow" I felt terribly sad.

We are a beautifully fragile species with pretty simple desires when it comes down to it: To be of worth. To be loved. To belong. And, sadly, that makes us prey to viruses.

I do hope these ex-NXIVM people find peace.

For my own part, I took a moment to send out a message to Mrs Dunbar - not that she'll be able to hear me obviously over the noise of the flames. I wanted her to know that I did indeed spend the week doing nothing. Not because I'm lazy. Not because I'm stupid. Not because I'm good for nothing. And not because I think I'm special, but because I'm human. And sometimes humans do get sick.

We don't have potpourri in our house. Mark is totally against it. He says whenever he sees a bowl of potpourri, it always makes him wonder what shit it's there to cover up the smell of.

Sometimes Mark is very wise.

Mar 26, 2023

WEE MARGARET'S BEAN CALENDAR

I had one of those 'holy shit" moments this week sitting down to write this blog, when I realized we are nearly in April. I can't believe how fast time is going. It feels like only yesterday I was complaining about it being Christmas already.

And now getting over last week's lurgy, I feel like I'm constantly doing catch-up. Watching me dither about the kitchen, my youngest told me not to stress. He said that I was just a little slow of thinking, and it wasn't as if I was operating under Wee Margaret's Bean Calendar. Surprised, I laughed out loud. My whole mood changed. Sometimes it's the weirdest of memories that change your perspective.

I should explain.

Several years ago, we had just moved into this house. Tweddley Manor had needed a full refurb and there was always something getting fixed somewhere or other and that made it ...uhm...interesting when you're trying to find keys or lost paperwork, or 'that thing' you'd put down for just a minute.

The kids had just gone back to school which was great on one hand, and terrible on the other. My youngest had resurrected his campaign against 10-year-olds doing homework ever, and my eldest seemed to have an ongoing slew of "really important' school projects that needed to be delivered in about half an hour.

I believe there are times when it is technically possible to demonstrate good textbook parenting. I also believe there are times to be a complete parenting shambles. That week had been more towards the shambles

We were all a bit nippy with one another, and when my eldest got snappy with me because I kept forgetting to refer to his 'nonbinary' friend as 'they' and not 'she', I snapped back and said, "Think yourself lucky. When I was growing up, my mother didn't believe that anyone was gay."

There'd then followed one of those silences that means there's explaining to do. My 10-year-old had put down his homework (any opportunity) and eyed me with earnest disbelief. My eldest, looking faintly disgusted, waited.

So I explained.

Where I grew up in Scotland pretty much everyone, lived in the same type of houses, was the same color of white, and men and women got married – or mysteriously remained single – and the only perceived difference between groups of people, was that some were Catholic and others were Protestant.

But when I went to drama school in Glasgow, nobody cared who was Catholic or Protestant – people were distinguished between who was gay and who was straight.

My mother could not understand this. "Men don't kiss men. And women are much too sensible for that sort of thing." she'd say.

I tried reasoning:
"Ok then, Liberace?"
"He's flamboyant. He's just a showman."

"What about Rock Hudson?"
"Not gay. Too tall."

"Alright then, Boy George."
"Don't be ridiculous. He's just a pop star. All pop stars dress up as girls. Don't you remember the 70s?"

I've pretty much always known I was heterosexual, but it seemed to me that not recognizing that some people were gay was bizarre – like not recognizing that some people have brown hair, or green eyes or are left-handed or right-handed. And I couldn't understand that my mother could not understand that, when she was someone who valued the truth so highly.

Years later after drama school, I took a job working in a gay bar with my friend, Strappy. Strappy is gay, and one of the smartest and most considered humans I know.

Strappy loved my mother, and my mother loved Strappy, and so one night when we were talking in the kitchen behind the bar, I told him about my frustration that my mother just didn't believe that homosexuality existed.

"It's just a matter of timing," he said. "She'll get there eventually. People are different. Some live in the here and the now, and use the Gregorian calendar. Others mean well, but take a while to catch up. And then those who live by Wee Margaret's Bean Calendar."

And we laughed.

Wee Margaret was a diminutive woman of indeterminate age who made the pub lunches during the week. Her calendar was a large pot that sat on the stove in the kitchen.

Every Monday, Wee Margaret would, with great effort, empty a giant can of beans in the pot and heat them up. After Monday lunch, there would be a line above the beans, showing the original cooking level. On Tuesday, she'd cook the same pot of beans, so after Tuesday lunch there would be two lines. As the week went on and more beans were served, there would be more lines. Strappy and I both knew people who only knew what day of the week it was after consulting Wee Margaret's Bean Calendar.

One night in the bar, Strappy was doing admin in the quiet of the kitchen, while I stood reading magazines in between periodic bartending.

Two men came in and ordered a Guinness and a gin and tonic. They hadn't been in the bar before, but I recognized them at the same time that they recognized me. It was my Mum's Minister, with the Assistant Minister. Though we all exchanged smiles, there was a moment where we all had an expression of "Oh holy crap."

As soon as they took their drinks and sat at a corner table, I hurried into the kitchen to tell Strappy what was going on. Strappy, puffing on a cigarette, was completely unfazed.

"Meh. We get Bishops in here. Rabbis. Even a couple of Archdeacons." he said.

"No," I stressed, "The point of it is that it's my Mum's Minister."

"No, the point of it," said Strappy, "That it doesn't matter who he is. This is a safe space for someone who currently doesn't have many safe places. You're freaked out? Believe me, he is more so. So, go out there and make sure he knows that he's alright."

So I went back out front. It was very quiet. There was nobody to serve, so I cleaned the bar.

And then all of the glasses.

And then I decided to wipe down the tables.

I had cleaned everything, but I still didn't know how to approach things or what to say.

So eventually, on the pretext of cleaning their table, I said to the Ministers, "I just want you to know that everything is totally cool, and that this is a safe space and...and I won't tell my Mum."

And my Mum's Minister smiled and asked, "Are you one of us as well?"

To which I replied nervously, "What? A Minister?"

They snorted with laughter, and then so did I.

Though I had promised him I wouldn't tell my Mum, I did. It came out in the middle of an argument. When she said, that she didn't know any real gay people, I told her she did.

It wasn't my proudest moment.

And yet it didn't surprise me at all, when she replied, "Well, that in no way changes the way I feel about him."

In the end, I was glad I told her.

In the late 80s, a gay Minister was still big news, and when the newspapers came after my Mum's Minister, my mother fought his corner with gusto.

"Wasn't he the same man who sat with your daughter? Wasn't he the same man who visited your father every week in hospital? What business is it of yours if he likes men or women? He's a good man, and a fantastic Minister."

"So," I'd told my kids, "If I'm honest, she didn't have a problem really, she just took a while to catch on. Like me, with the he, she, and they."

My 10-year-old hadn't really understood the story. He couldn't see why anybody would have a problem with anyone being gay. So, my teen explained that people used to be really against it, and that in some places some people still are.

"People who know what day it is by using Wee Margaret's Bean calendar."

Crisis averted, my 10-year-old had tried to concoct more reasons why he shouldn't have to do homework. I had resumed trying to find 'that piece of paper I'd just put down for five minutes.' And my eldest had wandered off to his computer to talk to someone much more groovier than me on Skype.

I heard him talking to his friend online.

"Dude," he said, "I am never eating beans in a restaurant again. ...Well, maybe on a Monday."

My youngest is no longer 10 but 15. It was five years ago I told them that story. Time really does fly. But then in some ways, in those past 5 years so much has happened, it's almost like another lifetime.

I guess, sometimes life is moving so fast it can feel like it's not moving at all. And sometimes you have to let go of where you're going, to take time to look back to see how far you've come. Then you can really recognize and appreciate change.

Otherwise you might find yourself having to work out what day of the week you're on, by the actions of a small woman, of indeterminate age, and a giant can of beans.

Apr 2, 2023

CELEBRATING WAFFLE MAKERS

The club that nobody wants to join.

I've always found radiology screening offices to be a bit like the setting of an Agatha Christie story.

There's the familiar cast in the waiting room: Receptionists, smiling and efficient, handing out forms to be filled in, like nothing bad in the world has happened recently or might happen any time soon.

There's the perfectly dressed organized lady, turning up for self-care. She dials down her anxiety, by continually texting, or writing notes. She stands up. She sits down. She flicks through the occasional magazine, with an air of forced invincibility

There's the older lady in a wheelchair, with her daughter or niece. They talk too loud. They both know time is likely on the short side for one of them, so they don't make space for sadness.

The terrified woman who found a lump on her breast and tried to ignore it. She hides in the corner, drowning in horrific visions of what it might be.

And there's me. Or someone like me.

When I was diagnosed with the big C, I got a message from my lovely friend, Bethany. Having navigated an intense journey with cancer herself, she wrote "Welcome to the club that nobody wants to join. Here however/whenever you need me."

I am forever grateful to her. It's the message I pass on to others who join our club. Then, if they ask, I tell them my journey: They found it, sorted it. It's all good. I have pills to take for a while, and I have a mammogram every 12 months and an ultrasound every 12 months - that way I'm never more than six months without a screening. But I'm clear. Free and clear.

This week was mammogram week and truth be told, I wasn't feeling the love.

My body decided it was done with the meds. It happens that way sometimes. Big sore mouth, cardboard body, lips like they've been Kardashianed, and tongue like the sole of an old slipper. It's not a huge big deal - there are other treatments - but it meant I wasn't feeling particularly perky.

In the changing room, eying my reflection in the mirror, I marveled that Mammogram capes have to be the only ones that don't let you feel like a superhero.

And then there I was, in the room with the big squeezy breast machine and a smart efficient breast tech in her 30s. I tried to look a little bright, or at least friendly, but it's just plain fact that when you feel like shit, you're not inclined to place your boobies in a waffle maker.

Clipboard in hand, she checked my details and we discussed what areas had to be scanned. She was very gentle and I realized that because I was so quiet she thought I was terrified. So I said, "Honestly just move me where you need me. I'm not scared to be here because a mammogram saved my life.

She smiled. A great wide smile.

"It saved my life too," she said.

So there we were: two members of The Club Nobody Wants To Join.

Her story was more a Tolkien novel rather than my, "Ladybird Guide to breast cancer," but happily we've both ended up on solid ground. Then she explained how afterwards she'd decided to become a mammogram tech because she wanted to show hope.

"I wish people would stop calling it "a battle," I said. "It's more a mystery. I've tried to muscle through these drugs that were clearly screwing with me because they seemed to be fine with everyone else on the planet. Like there was some kind of integrity to it. And I didn't want to be weak. And it's nothing frickin' personal. Your body does what your body does. And there's sometimes not much you can do about it."

"People say battle because they want you to feel brave and not scared," she said.

"Honestly, I mostly don't feel either," I said, "I'm just getting on with it."

"I reckon that's true for most of us," she replied

We did the exam, working to make sure the images were clear, and I actually learned stuff - apparently the tighter the squeeze of the machine, the less radiation used for imagery. Who knew?

"Thank you," I said when we finished. "I thought about calling it off today, because, well .. you know."

She nodded. "I do. No matter how you feel, nobody ever really wants to..."

"Stick their boobies in a waffle maker? No." I said.

We both laughed, and I told her I wasn't training to be a mammogram tech anytime soon. She said it really wasn't for everybody.

On the way out, I told the receptionists how wonderful she was. (Amazing how effusive you can be with a fat tongue.) They chuckled like I'd just given them a cake.

The efficient lady momentarily stood still, and the niece translated something in Spanish to the lady in the wheelchair, and I may have imagined it, but the woman hiding in the corner looked a tiny bit less terrified.

A few drug-free days and I'm feeling so much better.

And I keep thinking about the woman who did my scan.

I'm definitely not going to become a breast tech. I'm not technical that way, and besides, there's completely nothing that makes me want to get up close and personal to anybody's armpits, ever. But I do write a blog.

So I figured this week, I could tell you something that might be helpful.

A mammogram saved my life.

Apr 9, 2023

LETTER TO MY 16-YEAR-OLD SELF

43 Meadow View,
Cumbernauld, Glasgow

Dear 16-year-old self,

Ok, this is going to be a shocker, but Elton John is gay.
Yes he is. I don't care if he marries a woman. He's gay.

Oh and BTW (that means 'by the way' BTW) I know
you're worried because that Rangers supporting,
douchebag at school keeps yelling how you're a
lesbian. And you're bothered because, though you
don't think you are, he's so persistent he might be right.
It's OK. You don't like boys or really anyone that way yet.
Spoiler alert, your sexuality isn't decided by anyone
else. Especially by what people shout at you. Make a
mental note, Lynn, what people shout at you is
generally not the truth. The reason people shout is
because they really have nothing smart or inspiring to
say.

Although, while we're on the subject, bullying someone
for being a lesbian, makes as much sense as bullying
someone for having feet, or curly hair, or a dimple when
they smile.

There's nothing weird, shameful, or unnatural about homosexuality. The love of another person is the most wonderful gift in life, and the itinerary of their frontal pant area really has very little to do with that.

Right now, it feels like you'll be living in this little town and going to school forever. You won't. In 3 years' time, you'll be living and working in New York.

New York won't be easy. You'll witness drug addiction way too close, and what you see will put you off drugs forever. That is a good thing. People use all sorts of stuff to make them feel they're doing life properly. Don't bother with any of that. Dabble in whatever you fancy, by all means, but don't get too caught up in any of that posturing. The point of life is experience, why would you want to dumb that down?

Stand your ground. That sweet little funny guy you like, but don't want to sleep with, don't. His feelings will be hurt and you will feel bad, but instinct is an ally. That sweet little guy has something called "AIDS", a horrible new disease that, very soon, will seem unstoppable. In 5 years' time your smart, funny friend will be dead. Life is not fair. Don't expect it to be. And while you're still breathing, don't complain that it's not. But like I said before, instinct is your ally. Stop trying to ignore it.

Your heart will break a couple of times and (though each time you won't believe it) it really does work out for the best: These relationships are merely practice runs. You will meet 'the one' by chance.
You will know and so will he. And suddenly all those others will seem pointless.

You will lose your Mum and Dad and it will be excruciating and, even though you won't want to, you will keep breathing. You will tell yourself, they're not really gone, and they're just cruising around the Bahamas and don't have phone contact. But sometimes you will remember.

You will marry 'the one' and have two, quite perfect, sons who drive you crazy, but who keep you breathing when you remember about the Bahamas. You will worry about the world you bring them into. And honestly, that's understandable.

There will be times when the world will feel like it might have broken itself. There will be too much hate, and too much crazy and the most repugnant examples of humanity will appear to be in charge of everything at the very time when the earth needs help most.

Remind yourself, 16-year-old Lynn, that no matter how powerful these individuals paint themselves, no human is immortal, and the fate of the world really lies in the hopes and beliefs of those who are the same age you are now.

Be respectful of the young, Lynn. Remind yourself often that age is not a qualification, or a burden, but a luxury. The young will face trials specific to their own generation, Don't assume you always know the answer because you were their age once.

Oh, one more thing. There's this amazing invention – even more impressive than a video recorder – called a computer. And something called "the internet". These two things will change the world (and when I say that, I really mean it). You know how you used to wonder what people in history must have felt like when electricity was invented. You'll find out.

Anyway, back to Elton (I know, I can't believe I'm using him as a metaphor either). He's not only gay, he's happy. But to be that he's had to weather a lot of storms. Some people love him, and some people don't, and he is OK with that, because he is happy in his skin.

Be as honest with yourself as you can bear to be, 16-year-old self, and you'll be your own best friend. Lie, and you will always be your own worst enemy. And remember to be kind to people you meet along the way because, even when you don't agree, they're trying to find a way to navigate their best life too. Integrity is its own reward and stupid is as stupid does, and the right of the individual to be able to make mistakes and learn from them is vital.

Lastly, the big event of the year (aside from your 16th birthday) is that Prince Charles is going to marry Lady Diana Spencer. They're going to have a much bigger party, but you're going to have a much better time.

Yours sincerely,

Fiftysomethingyearold -Lynn Xox

AVOIDING THE HUMP

I was very tall for a teenager - especially a Scottish teenager - and used to slouch a lot. This worried my mother greatly. Concerned I might develop a hump, she decided I should do a modeling class in Glasgow to learn how to walk properly.

I've never been modeling material, but I'm not against it - though I couldn't comprehend what my classmates were training to model for other than maybe the 1950s. And that is why in class when we were practicing runway walking, I was often to be found muttering "Oh for fucking fuck's sake" under my breath when it was my turn to strut and swish across the room. (Though not as under my breath as I'd hoped, it turned out.)

My mother was advised, in no uncertain terms, that as I was 'a bit of a character', I would be more suited to the speech and drama classes held by the same company.

The speech and drama classes turned out to be of a fairly similar flavor. All my classmates were female and dressed in varying shades of pink.

The speech part of class consisted of reading poetry out loud and the drama came from getting a critique afterward on delivery and posture. (Turns out some people don't like not being perfect.)

Now, I like poetry (not all of it obviously - I'm not completely crazy) but I was dismayed to discover that Edward Lear and Ogden Nash were not considered poets, and neither was Brecht because he was too angry apparently.

For the purposes of class, poetry seemed to be exclusively written by women called Emily, and covered such topics as flowers and birds and femininity and loveliness.

(Honestly, after a couple of weeks I was almost homesick for the strutting and swishing.)

There was one girl who distinguished herself from the others by wearing black. Her parents were very well-to-do, and she seemed to get away with a lot more. With blunt rebelliousness, she would stand up to read some poem about loveliness and then do a quick switch and resolutely drop into Sylvia Plath.

This was hilarious on two fronts: One because of the gasps of shock around the room, and two, because there are some poems that sound hilarious in a Scottish accent.

"You dooo not dooo, you dooo not dooo. Any more, black shooe. In which I have lived like a foooot."

Unfortunately, she didn't stay for too long.

I could handle the pink, but I really struggled to find anything to recite that didn't sound exactly the same as everyone else was reciting. (I mean how many lovely flowers, birds, and urns can you take?)

Perhaps because they thought just plain old words on a page was too much for my pretty little head, I was offered a book of poetry with pictures in it - The Fireside Book of David Hope - and told to "find something in that."

And that is how I landed on reciting a poem called "My Special Day" about an older lady who is having a birthday.

It began: "I watched as the postman drew nearer my door, in anticipation of presents in store."

I don't remember the next line, but the line after that I do,

"Because birthdays are special when you're 64."

That line is ingrained in my mind because the teacher was very particular as to how it should be stressed. I had to repeat it often, to get it absolutely right.

Because birthdays ARE special. Birthdays ARE special.

She was very insistent. My teenage mind wondered if it was because she was 64. I wasn't sure - under the bright lipstick and bouffant hairspray she really could have been any age. Maybe she'd read a survey that revealed that 64 was THE birthday to have.

What I did know is that when I said it the way she liked - as if I was talking to a frickin' idiot, frankly - she would clasp her hands together and smile most appreciatively. And my classmates would marvel like I'd just managed a particularly difficult gymnastic feat at the Olympics.

There was no ignoring it. I was completely a fish out of water. They knew it and I knew it.

I suppose I could have pushed my mother into letting me leave, but I liked traveling into Glasgow, and I especially liked occasionally sneaking into bars after class for a small spot of underage drinking. (Yes I know it was wrong but consider Pernod and Blackcurrant its own punishment).

Also, if I'm honest, over the weeks I learned to like these people. Each Saturday was like going to a foreign country where everybody spoke some strange incomprehensible language, even though the words they used were still English. But they weren't bad people. They meant no harm. For all their pink and posturing and completely ridiculous pronunciations, we weirdly accepted each other.

Besides when I managed the couplet at the end in the same class style - the tone a heady mix of patronizing and slightly deranged -

 "My daughter was calling a half-world away. To tell me she loves me on My Special Day"

- the teacher would wipe a tear from her eye and my charmingly clad classmates would applaud with such gusto that it was hard not to be proud.

Admittedly knowing that the relationship was distinctly short-term, made the whole thing easier. As with anything, once you know it won't last forever, it's wise to make space to enjoy the good parts.

When I left class I never met up with them again. I did wave to one of them once, across a busy street one Saturday night in Glasgow. I was rough and ready for a stand-up gig and she was beautifully coiffed in shades of tan and fuchsia. But we both smiled warmly.

Though I still am way too slouchy, my mother was right. Sending me to these classes probably did stop me getting the hump. About many things.

Also, it was my birthday last week and it was lovely. Even though I'm in my 50s, it really was a special day.

I can't imagine how amazing 64 is going to be.

Apr 23, 2023

WHEN CHICKENS CURSE

Letting it fly

Last month I planted a ton of seeds in trays: red peppers, eggplants, and various types of tomatoes. On reflection, I might have been just the tiniest bit over-enthusiastic, because the whole load of those fuckers grew. Now I have to work out what to do with them all. I've given a ton to friends and neighbors. I've planted even more, yet still, they haunt me.

Tomatoes are fairly easy to get rid of - though not to the extent that I planted. As for red bell peppers - come on who doesn't like red bell peppers? Well, bloody loads of people apparently.

So that's why I was out in the front yard this week pottering around and trying to think of what I could do with them all.

"Hello there!"

I turned and saw a sweet wee lady standing at the gate. I don't know her to speak to, but I do know she lives in the neighborhood as she often passes by Tweddley Manor on her morning walk.

Smiling, she asked about our chickens. Seems that when she passed by on her walk she loved the sound of the chickens in our backyard, because it reminded her of her childhood in Chile. But she was worried we might have lost our rooster as she hadn't heard him crow for a while.

I explained that Genghis is fine and just isn't particularly crowy. She looked visibly relieved and said that as she hadn't seen the rooster sitting on the wall for the longest time, she thought he might have died.

It took a moment for the penny to drop, but once it did, I laughed.

I should explain. We hatched most of our chickens, and as such you don't get to choose what one is male and female. One of the eggs we hatched was a rooster called Pegs. Though he was the biological son of Genghis, his genes must have skipped a generation, because while Genghis veers more towards the chartered accountant of the chicken world, Pegs was absolutely the poultry version of Ivan the Terrible. He was all cock and attitude. When he wasn't trying to cause a mutiny within the coop, he used to love to fly up and land on the side wall crowing a blatant "fuck a doodle doo" to anyone passing by.

That was the rooster she was talking about. The one she apparently found charming.

It was never going to work out with Pegs and Genghis so we had to let him go. A good friend of mine keeps a ton of chickens on a ranch out of town, and Pegs was the perfect fit (after some adjustments).

A normal rooster likes to take care of around 10 hens - basically, then he doesn't over-shag them. Pegs apparently needed 20, and even then at one point tried to escape in order to *take care* of the hens in the next coop. But he's happier there. The move was right for him.

Anyway, all of that seemed to be a bit complicated to explain to my new Chilean pal, so instead I just told her to wait a minute, and went off to fetch her some eggs.

When I handed her the egg box she looked at me like I'd just given her the keys to my car.

"Ohmigod. What can I give you in return? she said.

"Nothing, " I replied. "Consider it a gift from the rooster."

"I have citrus. You want citrus.?"

"Don't worry. Honestly."

"But I must give something in return"

"Ooh, I have an idea. " I said, "Hang on." I hurried off and picked up a couple of potted tomatoes.

"Take these. please." I said. "Honestly, you're doing me a favor"

She was a little astonished, and maybe a little overwhelmed. She thanked me most effusively, and headed off home.

I smiled. Her joy was infectious. And it's always nice to make a new pal. Then I headed back to my plants, annoyed with myself for not making her take some peppers as well.

It made me happy to think of Pegs. He really was so full-on. And so arrogant when he sat on the wall, yelling assorted curse words in chicken language to passersby.

I had been so sad at the time to let him go - I'd hatched him from an egg. But there are times in life when you have to accept what is, rather than what was. Whenever I get updates on Peg's antics, or videos of him trying to lead a coup, it is so clear that he is much happier there than he would have been here.

Letting go has been on my mind a lot of late.

I let go of my preventative cancer drugs. It's not a bad thing. They really didn't agree with me, and I'll definitely be a lot healthier without them. I just have to accept that a pill isn't the same as a promise, and in the life of all grown-ups there really are no guarantees.

And work-wise, I've also let go. Last year I agreed with Mark that I probably wouldn't ever go back to teaching group story classes. As magical as it is to see and hear people come out of themselves and tell a story to an audience - the logistics of teaching the course just don't work while I'm juggling so many other things. So, we adapted the course to be online and this week we sent it out onto Udemy.

It's the beginning of a beautiful thing and I'm proud of it, but there's an ending there too. I hatched that course, though admittedly Mark is the one who truly made it beautiful. Now I have to let it fly. I suspect like Pegs, it will be a better fit in its new home. I still do believe everybody needs to learn and appreciate their own story, but maybe they don't all have to do it in a theatre in front of an audience.

I cleaned up in the front yard and headed indoors. I had more letting go to do. After more than three years of silliness, we were recording the last episode of our podcast FHH. Neil, Ches, and I started doing it in the days of the pandemic because...well, because. It was all remote - Chesney and I didn't even meet Neil in the flesh until series 3 and we were podcasting live at the Edinburgh Fringe.

Now we've grown from podcast mates to proper mates, and though the only thing we'll really lose is the legitimate reason for meeting online on a Tuesday morning to talk for hours. It's still a little sad. But it's the right thing to do. It's time. Growth means change. We all feel it.

I finish the recording and head back out into the front yard. There's a huge box of citrus fruits just inside the front gate. There's lemons and some oranges and these frickin' MASSIVE citrussy things called Pomelos. If you don't know what they are, picture grapefruits the size of footballs.

A gift. A beautiful gift from my new Chilean friend. She was only a little woman. Moving that size of stuff takes determination. I'm frankly pretty astonished.

While one story was ending, another story had already begun. Seems like we all have to move things and make room. My melancholy moved to gratitude. Looking at the size of these pomelos, I'm glad my problem is just seedlings.

I pick up the box and lay it next to the pepper plants. There really is quite a bit of citrus there. I wonder. Now what?

Apr 30, 2023

GOATS VERSUS BATMAN

I nearly bought a goat last week, but my youngest talked me out of it.

Wandering into the living room - no doubt considering how to persuade me to 'fess up where I'd stashed the Oreo cookies - he caught me studying my phone and asked what I was doing - not expecting the answer I gave.

"Woah. Are you talking animal goat, or are you talking like G.O.A.T ?" he asked, in that exact age-specific tone of 15-year-old.

"Animal goat. What other kind of goat is there?" I replied.

He snorted. "Sometimes you're a bit out of touch, Mom"

"Most of the time, probably," I said, browsing a lovely selection of goats on my phone.

"And is there some reason we should be getting a goat?" he asked - way too judgmentally.

"Absolutely!" I replied doing my best to sound intellectually superior. "They give you milk and uhm mohair and uhm... other stuff"

His eyes narrowed. "Is this for Dad's birthday?"

I said nothing.

"You know, you could just get him a hat or some pairs of socks?

"We get him that every year?"

"That's what he likes. And also, no we don't. Last year we got him a bee hive. "

"Exactly." I said " And he loves it. So I thought this year maybe he would like a goat. Goats are fabulous. And I just got this message about some goats that need rescuing as their owner is moving, so they're selling them off really cheap. Dad could get a goat and socks and maybe a hat as well."

My youngest stood beside the sofa, saying nothing. (Honestly, even though he's my child and I love him, it was pretty annoying - him just standing there was taking all the joy out of flicking through photographs of lovely goats on my phone.)

"The Oreos are in the yellow tub in the cupboard next to the oven," I said.

"Good, thanks," he said and continued to stand there.

I sighed and put down my phone. "What?"

"Do we have room for a goat?" he asked

"Probably. Maybe." I said, trying to sound intellectually superior.

"Do we have room for two goats though, because goats don't like to be on their own? Look it up. They get unhappy on their own. "

I did a quick search on goat happiness and Goddamit he was right. Bloody goats and their social neediness. One goat would be a push. Two goats impossible. And it doesn't matter what the occasion is, you can't own an animal if by doing so that animal would suffer. It has to be a win-win for you and the animal both.

I heaved a huge defeated sigh.

"They have hats and socks and stuff at Target." my youngest said, "And also a good return policy, which is helpful when you're buying for Dad."

I nodded assent. Goat crisis averted - my youngest went off to raid the Oreo stash.

My husband Mark is a wonderful wonderful human, but he is notoriously shit at birthdays. He struggles finding the right present for anyone because he wants it to be perfect, but he's picky so nothing really is perfect, and so present buying is not one of his stronger points.

But his own birthday is the worst because he's quite happy just being regularly contented throughout the year. So, the idea that he has to find more happy for one day of the year, when he's already quite happy enough as it is, ties his head in knots.

Mark is three years younger than me. We met when I was 35 and he was 32 and both our birthdays are in April. It wasn't long before the birthday thing became clear. Though he would stress about getting me the absolutely right thing for my birthday, he really couldn't be bothered remembering anything about his - including his own age. So the year I was 38, I just told him he was 38 too. When he turned 38 for three years running, it dawned on him. He felt a little cheated that he 'never got to be 36 or 37' and has resolutely kept a marker on his own age from then on.

And he does now, in fact, have a method of dealing with birthdays. Mostly he tries to ignore them hoping they might go away, and then has a last-minute panic.

I am his polar opposite. Ooh, I do like a birthday. I like the cakes and the candles and the bad singing and the presents, but mostly I love the excuse for letting people know that you love them. It doesn't have to be expensive - and in fact most of the time I prefer it when it's not. It's best of all when it involves a wee bit of daftness.

Over the years we've learned to find a happy medium - or at least remind ourselves that a happy medium is the goal. I have to remind myself that each person is allowed to celebrate their birthday the way they want to, and he has to remind himself that birthdays do exist. The only time it becomes really tricky is when it's his birthday.

I don't want him to have a lovely birthday just because I like birthdays. I want him to have a lovely birthday because he's a really wonderful man.

After my discussion with Lachlan though, I realized that this year, I wasn't sticking to my side of the bargain. So I took the bull by the horns and brought up the B word with Mark and asked him what he really wanted to do.

Turns out he wanted homemade burgers and fries, and maybe a cake and just hanging with the four of us, and that for him that was special enough.

So, while Mark pottered about in the goat-free backyard, the boys and I went to Target and bought a selection of men stuff that may be worn or may not be worn. - But that's ok because - as Lachlan reminded me - Target has a fabulous return policy.

It was a lovely birthday. Laid back and easy, and dare I say, happy. (possibly apart from when he was modeling a new hat, and I said he looked good for 58 and he eyed me and stated, most pointedly, that he knew exactly what age he was.)

I didn't buy a goat. I did order a bat box from Amazon though.

Lachlan eyed it lying amongst the pile of Target gifts.

"What's that for?" he asked.

"Bats."

His eyes narrowed. "Ok. So, are you buying bats?" he asked way too suspiciously for a 15-year-old.

"No you don't buy bats, they're just around." I smiled. "I got them this house in case they want to move in."

"Why do you want bats?"

"Dad likes bats. They eat mosquitoes."

He nodded, dare I say it faintly impressed. "Cool," he said.

I guess the thing about birthdays is that whatever way you do it, the point is it's a celebration of you. So, if it was your birthday recently, or if it's your birthday soon, may it in some way be a reminder that the world is so very glad you're here.

And also, just so you know, I know a place where you can get goats. Really nice goats. Though obviously it's a two-goat minimum.

May 7, 2023

EARWIGGERY

It is a small world after all.

Oooh it's been the battle of the earwigs this week in Tweddley Manor. These creepy crawly wee douchebags are determined to destroy my seedlings, and I am just as determined they will not win. And they're everywhere. Seems like they're bloody Universal, able to transcend time and space in the most frickin' irritating manner.

Years ago, when dinosaurs still roamed the earth and I was maybe in my first or second year at school in Scotland, I'd gone to my Nana's for lunch. My Nana was a capable woman with standards - one of which was that she absolutely did not under any circumstances approve of bad language. Yet, I remember her coming across an earwig hiding in a box of eggs and she let out a sequence of vowels and consonants that sounded remarkably sweary.

And just this week in Tweddley Manor, I heard the most manly of boys I live with let out a very unmanly squeal having opened the mailbox and found 4 big fat ones sitting in there. I have as yet never met anyone who likes earwigs. I'm not even sure earwigs like earwigs.

So, I sat down to write a blog about our ongoing battle with them, and then something kept repeating in my mind. I was sure I must have written about them before.

I looked up my notes, and low and behold this time three years ago, they were very much on my mind - and on my seedlings.

It was May 2020, and life was very different for all of us. But reading through what I'd written, it seemed what mattered to me most was exactly the same.

****

May 2020

I was pottering about the backyard this morning, drinking tea, and surveying who was winning the battle of Tweddle versus earwigs.

Hubster, Mr Tweddle has planted a variety of vegetables for our delectation, but the earwigs have been voraciously delecting them instead. I won't lie. It's been tense. Mr Tweddle, armed with earwig traps, a sprayer filled with washing liquid, and a determined expression, heads out to the backyard every night around sunset.

Because earwigs, like all of the bleakest challenges, are much more powerful in the dark.

I'm halfway through a six-week course of radiotherapy and have found myself unreasonably tired. (I say unreasonably because - even though they told me at the beginning of this to expect fatigue, I'd decided they meant other people and not me.)

I told the doctor last week how tired I was, and he smiled. Then I informed him that I was having to sleep an actual full 8 hours at night and then would even have a nap in the afternoon just to get by. He grinned and said I should be proud of how well I was doing.

That was the worst. Actual fucking grinning. And the pride bit? I'm from Cumbernauld. We don't do pride at the best of times, let alone when we're vulnerable.

Over at the vegetable patch, the earwigs seemed to have gained ground on the kale and cauliflower, but Tweddles have regained eggplants and peppers. Mr Tweddle would be pleased.
I sipped some tea and stopped beside the random pomegranate tree that we didn't plant but grew anyway.

When we'd moved to this house, there was a large dead pomegranate tree. There was so much risk of it falling on someone, that sadly, it had to be chopped down. Yet a year later the tree just reappeared, because the root system was strong enough, it completely regrew.

The doctor had told me how much he loved British people and he was reading a book about Winston Churchill and the 2nd World War. I'd laughed and said I was glad he was reading something lightweight. I'd thought about telling him about the earwigs but, for some reason, a story about my Mum had come out of my mouth instead.

When she was about 8, the air raid sirens had gone off when she was at school, and the whole class had to run across the playground to get to the shelter. They were all terrified that a bomb was going to get them when they were running, but they managed to get to the shelter safe and sound. After the raid, they re-emerged from the shelter and a whole side of the street was nothing but rubble. Everything she knew had changed.

The doctor had cleared his throat and there was a bit of a pause. Then we'd shaken our heads and muttered stuff about living through difficult times. Then a little tearfully I'd blurted out that I couldn't stop feeling a bit lost.

And he'd nodded and quietly said, "We all do."

The May morning sun was beautiful today. The pomegranate tree that came back from the dead looked spectacular - all shiny green leaves, and defiant bright red flowers. It cared nothing for the hardship of the past, was unyielding to the vagaries of earwig war, and focussed solely on the business of growing its spectacular new life.

I know I have to be careful. I do. Not so much with my body, but with my head.
I don't want to be going to a medical facility every day. I don't want to be having radiotherapy. In my head, I was done with this shit a long time ago. But it has to be dealt with. There's no other way. And I can handle it. Totally. But I must stay in my own story.

It's so tricky though because there are earwigs.

When I hear those crazy conspiracies about 5G, or lizards, or black ops, or see individuals I thought I knew, loudly losing their shit on social media because they've been asked to wear a piece of cloth over half their face when buying groceries, I lose myself. I enter into a different story. Their story. The one where they're talking about thinning out the weak in the herd. And I realize that the weak they're talking about is me.

All around the backyard this morning, plants were showing off their blooms. The flowers on the pomegranate tree that we didn't plant but got anyway, were defiantly bright.

The earwigs have gained ground on the kale and cauliflower, but we Tweddles have regained eggplants and peppers. Though the battle sometimes feels relentless, the Tweddles have resilience, determination, and access to bug control, and thus will ultimately come through this victorious.

I slept a full 10 hours last night, and this morning I got up already accepting I'll nap this afternoon.

And it's OK. In fact, it's fine. Because I know to my core, that in the future there'll be some big fucking defiant flowers.

****

I looked out the window after reading that and noticed the pomegranate tree. Three years later and it is tall and strong and blooming with flowers. Ridiculously so.

Like earwigs, challenge is cyclical. It's nothing personal. It goes around and around, and sometimes it's your turn.

It is inevitable, and at points, almost completely overwhelming. But it does eventually move on.

So, wherever you are, whatever part of the cycle you're in, congratulate yourself on your strength. You've come far.

We are all in some stage of blooming most defiantly.

May 14, 2023

THREE TIMES A SUNDAY

It's a Mother of a Day

Today I am fairly certain I will become the owner of two new Hibiscus plants. I say that because that's what I've told my kids to get me. I didn't even subtly drop hints. I just said, "Dudes, it's Mother's Day all over America this Sunday and I need two red Hibiscus plants for the front yard. You can get them at the Home Depot. Maybe get your Dad to take you." Message received, they both nodded their assent, grateful that we're all on the same page.

Yes, I know it's probably not how a woman is supposed to do Mother's Day. I expect I'm meant to be doing something lady-like like swooning over chintz fabric to make lovely little throw cushions or some crap like that, gasping with surprise when my kids appear with some flower/balloon display combo proclaiming their undying love. But we're really not that kind of family. If I'm honest, I'm not convinced anybody is that kind of family.

I'm not a big fan of the Mother's Day thing - though for selfish reasons, I'm not entirely against it - Oh come on, who doesn't like getting stuff? My issue is that for a day that's supposed to be about celebration, too many people experience alienation.

Because families are not all created equal. Fact.

I know I've been very lucky. I loved my mother very much, and she me. And I in turn have two sons I love very much, and they me. But, you don't have to be Freud to recognize that 'mothering' in terms of a topic is not universally simple.

I know people who are struggling with infertility, some who have lost children, same-sex families, and blended families where the right mother to celebrate can be a bit of a political minefield. People who've been abandoned by their mothers. Mothers who are estranged from their offspring. That's a whole lot of issues right there that you won't find in poetic form in the middle of your average Hallmark card.

And honestly, I'm not even sure I am a proper mother. Yes I did all that biological stuff that qualifies me, but in some ways, Mark is better at mothering roles than me: doctors appointments, school councils, anything involving form filling or timetabling or driving to and from, that's him. But he's not a lady, so his mothering skills are not celebrated today. He gets Father's Day to be equally awkward about.

Parenting-wise, I'm more the cuddles, the 'big talks', the taking care of when sick, the hot dinners, the 'Do you currently feel you're being the best version of yourself?" conversations. If that counts as mothering, then sure, I do that.

Historically, I did try to downplay Mother's Day one year, but it didn't work. Because I completely ignored it, both boys did too, and I was surprisingly offended.

So that Sunday afternoon, I called a meeting in the living room and stated that as it seemed there'd been a vote in the house to completely ignore card-giving days, I expected this meant I could completely ignore both their birthdays and Christmas as well. That sorted that shit out pronto.

It would be nice if these days that we know are kind of bullshit didn't actually affect us. But the real shit is that they do.

We have one custom we do as a family every birthday/holiday/special event that I love called the three things. We sit together at the dinner table or in the living room and each one of in turn has to say:

> 1. What we are grateful for.
>
> 2. Something that we love, like, or respect in each of the other people in the group.
>
> 3. Something we did today that we are proud of.

Yes, I know that might seem ridiculously touchy-feely, but doing those three things together as a family has not just seen us through special events, they've also helped us keep our heads above water during some pretty horrific times. Because no matter what three things are said, they remind us that we are part of something, and we belong.

So, later today there's a very high likelihood of getting two Hibiscus plants and I'll totally act shocked and surprised because I am not a heathen. Also, I've got a laundry to put on, and I have to feed and walk the dog. Then, I'll potter about the kitchen making a late brunch, and maybe later on I'll potter about the garden. Then probably sometime around dinner time we'll sit together and do the three things, and then we'll wander off into our lives again.

If you're struggling with today, you could do worse than trying the three things with people you see as your family, in person, or on a call. And if any one of those people tries to make you feel like you're being a big softy by suggesting it, guilt trip them into submission. That's what I always do.

Because today, like every day, you do have a right to feel you belong.

May 21, 2023

TONE DEAF

Full-blown confession: I listen to Classic FM in the morning. If you've never heard of Classic FM, that will be because you are a much groovier individual than me. It's a UK-based radio station that plays classical music, and I do like me a bit of Brahms or Handel or Grieg, or a cheeky wee blast of Stravinsky when I open my eyes on the world.

I blame this love of classical music partly on my Mum's wee brother, Uncle James, but mostly on a lady called Mrs Rennie, who taught choir at my school. Mrs R was one of those truly extraordinary teachers who appear once or twice in a lifetime. I don't know if she realized how brilliant she was, because she was so busy actually being brilliant. But, she firmly believed that everybody had something to offer, and was forever telling me I had a lovely voice.

That's why, one year when we were rehearsing for the Christmas concert in the local church, she decided I would sing a wee solo piece in the middle of *Ding Dong Merrily On High*. Even thinking about it all these years later sends a shiver down my spine. I mean, Ding Dong Merrily On Fucking High. If you've never heard that particular Christmas carol, you have been very lucky. It's bloody awful.

Unsurprisingly, I really really didn't want to do it. I was 10 years old and wanted to fit in with the choir like everyone else. But Mrs Rennie wouldn't hear of it. Despite her assurances that I had perfect pitch, I was so anxious I couldn't sleep.

As it was approaching Christmas, I figured I could mention to God that if he didn't want to completely ruin his son's birthday, he needed to find a way that I didn't have to sing. And lo and behold, the night before the choir concert there was a massive snowfall and the concert was canceled. Hallelujah, a proper Christmas miracle.

Years later I discovered Mrs Rennie was right though and I do actually have a pretty good ear for music. I was in a fancy play with the Royal National Theatre and the end of the first half was me singing a folk song in a meaningful way, accompanied by a mandolin.

One night however, I positioned myself for the song, but when I turned to nod to the mandolin player for us to begin, I saw only an empty chair where a guy playing a stringed instrument should be.

I paused for a moment, clearing my throat in my most "Where the fuck are you?" tone. But to no avail. I had no choice. So, hoping to drown out the frantic backstage panic as they hunted for the errant musician, I began to sing.

Halfway through my second verse, a very ruffled mandolin player was unceremoniously propelled onto the stage, and began playing in the key he was used to playing in. Extraordinarily, it turned out that it was the exact key I was singing in. A proper Christmas miracle - except it was June.

After the show, people marveled at my perfect pitch and scowled at the mandolin player. He defensively claimed he'd been taken off guard by a particularly sturdy and problematic bowel movement - though we were all convinced he'd just been off somewhere smoking a joint.

Anyway, I've recently had to do without Classic FM for a couple of weeks. It had proclaimed itself to be the station of The Coronation and was all full of pomp and pageantry for the then-future king.

It's not just that I'm Scottish or that I'm not big into the Royals, but I had problems getting my head around the fact that 100 million pounds of public money was to be spent on two humans riding along in a golden carriage and putting priceless jewels on their heads to celebrate their incoherent specialness, when so many many people are struggling financially.

If you enjoy Royals, good for you, I'm glad somebody got something out of it. We don't all have the same taste. Some people, for example, think Ding Dong Merrily On Fucking High is a lovely Christmas carol. For me, I felt sick to my stomach.

I did my best to avoid it, in the news and on Classic FM.

And maybe the change of routine was part of the reason I was so out of sorts when a friend went a bit mental this week. It was ugly and hurtful and I was on the verge of responding in a way I don't like, when the thought entered my head that I could take a moment and not make it about me. I asked my friend if there was something I could do to help and the whole story came tumbling out. They were dealing with stuff that could topple even the strongest of grown adults. Ashamed and overwhelmed, they were doing it alone, and the words coming out of their mouth were from pain rather than aggression. I had misheard.

Goddamit, and there was me with my perfect pitch too.

It's true that the sounds we make, don't always line up with the way others hear them.

Words can be thoughtless rather than willfully damaging, yet the end result can be the same. Like the friend who always posts pictures of her delectable pool house, or the couple who are always so much in love, or the humblebrag about money or awards or general specialness. They're decent people who wish to be seen as 'part of' rather than 'better than' but that's not always how it comes across.

Even in Notes From the Valley there must be times when you who read it, and want to punch me in my smug Scottish face for my charming wee vignettes.

We are all off-key some of the time.

But words are different from actions. Technically it didn't matter whether the mandolin player professed to a solidly problematic bowel movement or confessed he was just smoking a joint. Either way, he didn't turn up.

It sucks to be left feeling like the idiot, but my choice was to explain it away or do what I knew to be right.

This morning on Classic FM - the station of the Coronation - the leading news story was about the increase of mothers in the UK stealing formula milk, because they can't afford to feed their babies.

Maybe I should listen to jazz in the mornings.

May 28, 2023

DEFENDING THE DONUT WALL

It was Lachlan's birthday this week and despite my protestations, the Tweddle Donut Wall was ignored in favor of a cake. I'm not going to lie, I was pretty disappointed.

I mean, who doesn't love a donut wall? It's simultaneously delicious and ridiculous. It says, "Have a donut from this marvelous display!"

Hand on heart, I can honestly say, donut walls never fail to make me happy and I can't even eat the bloody donuts.

And we've used it for Lachlan's birthday every year since he turned 11.

His 10th birthday party was a fairly crazy affair. Cancer was a nagging doubt in the back of my mind. I knew there had been something found in the mammogram, but I was waiting for the biopsy and decided to distract myself with an awesome birthday party.

He had a cupcake tower, and a bouncy water slide, and a petting zoo which consisted of a snake or two and some bored-looking rabbits.

Lachlan has always loved animals, and more than anything, he wanted a dog. Mark and I weren't against it, but we didn't know what the score was going to be with my health, so we persuaded him to wait.

Not for your birthday, but maybe for Christmas....?

After the diagnosis, I'd told his teenage brother as practically as I could. Though he was really upset, I said that if he could promise me he would handle his homework, I would promise him I would handle the cancer. We had a brief stoic handshake and a long tearful cuddle, and then we moved on.

But I couldn't work out how to tell Lachlan. He was too young to be dealing with any of this. He still cuddled with his toy from his toddler days (called Neil The Seal) when he slept and insisted I say goodnight to both of them when I tucked him in.

Then one day, we were all hanging out as a family, laughing about Mark's so-called adoration of Home Depot.

When we laugh together, everything seems possible. I said to the family I had an announcement.
I said that I felt I should say sorry because I thought I'd been crankier than usual of late. I explained it was because I was not very well and that I'd have to go to hospital.
But after the hospital, I'd come home again and I'd be fine. And my 10-year-old cheered, because all he heard was that I was going to be fine.

He couldn't have given me a better gift.

My first surgery was plain sailing. Nobody liked it, but we handled it. I was sick and I got better. Homework was handed out and mostly it got done. And maybe by Christmas, we'd get a dog.

The second surgery in December was much tougher. When the infection hit, everything was pretty scary. I will never forget the look on the face of the little 10-year-old man who stood by my bedside, half raging, half sobbing, "You are not to do this again, you understand. No more hospitals. No more surgery. We are all meant to be having Christmas. Promise me you will not do this again!" before crumpling into a tearful snuggle.

By February I was better. The whole "Mom's not well" topic of conversation had pretty much disappeared, apart from when the subject of getting a dog came up. Mark suggested that it would be best if we waited until Mom was fully back to health again. And I said nothing, knowing that the third surgery was a given.

When I got the date, I sat down with my eldest. He was anxious, but he understood.
With Lachlan, I was scared. I had made him a promise that I'd known I couldn't keep.

But one night we were taking selfies together on his phone with Neil The Seal. We were both howling with laughter at how Neil The Seal looked terrified and adorable in all the pictures. And nothing – nothing in the world – feels so brilliant as sharing a really good hearty laugh with a 10-year-old kid.

So I took a breath and told him - that I had to break my promise and have one more surgery. He looked at me, saying nothing, his face holding a very similar expression to Neil The Seal. I promised that it honestly wouldn't be as bad as the last one.

He shook his head. Then he sighed heavily. Then said, "I am just never going to get a dog, am I?" in a way that made us both howl again with laughter.

The surgery went fine and 10 days before his 11th birthday, we adopted Arthur, a 2-year-old terrier mix of dubious heritage from the East Valley Rescue. Lachlan loved Arthur from the moment he set eyes on him.

And he planned his own 11th birthday party. He decided on a very specific group of guests – both kids and adults that he likes. We had a bouncy water slide, and a trampoline (for dry bouncing), a motorized car, and a little soccer area. He ordered pizza from his favorite pizza place and of course in the center of it all, the donut wall.

This year is different.

This year we'll have cake. This year the donut wall is relegated to the back of the cupboard. Lachlan is no longer little. He is 16 years old and he completely knows his own mind. Neil The Seal still has a place in his bedroom, but now you'll find him on a shelf rather than cuddled up by the pillow. And I am healthy, and have no surgeries at all planned.

I asked him what he wanted for his birthday. I suggested maybe a bouncy slide or water balloons or a games party or a movie day. He thought it over for a while and then responded "Nah." He wanted cake and take-out pizza from the local Italian place and just us and Arthur. "Let's make it chill. Who you love is everything. The rest is just frosting."

True.

Still, who doesn't love a big donut wall?

June 4, 2023

SOCK IT TO ME

Michelangelo - everyone's wee arty pal

I like Michelangelo - though despite what my kids might tell you, I'm not old enough to know him personally. Anyway, I like him and I think it's universally agreed that he was quite a talented guy. But by his own words, not perfect. He's quoted as saying that meaning and expression are found through the pursuit of perfect imperfection.

I tried knitting socks for a friend once, and miraculously we're both still friends: They were bloody impossible to knit and I spent very many expletive-filled evenings persevering, only to deliver what were - at best - pretty poor excuses for foot coverings. Charitably, she received my gift of socks with exactly the right mix of reserved gratitude and compassion, with just a touch of abject horror thrown in.

So, I was mighty impressed this weekend when my friend Anne dropped in with socks her mother had knitted for Mark and me. Not only are they recognizably proper socks, they fit perfectly.

I marveled at Anne's Mum's ability to create such a thing. If you look closely you can see they've been handmade. You have to look hard though because they're pretty much perfect. I unreservedly love them.

When I was a kid I sneered at homemade things, and I blame this almost entirely on a BBC children's TV program called Blue Peter. Every week on this program, they'd have a 'craft segment' during which they made monstrous assaults to the eye such as 'lovely flower vases from old washing up liquid bottles and some sticky back plastic'. Every bloody week there was something with an old washing-up liquid bottle and some sticky back plastic. This may, indeed, have been a gift to the environment but was a catastrophe for interior design. Not only that, everything they made was totally impractical.

I kid you not, every Christmas on Blue Peter they made a lantern out of old wire coat hangers, tinsel, and some candles that even as a six-year-old I could tell was a massive fire risk. My little mind used to wonder if they just didn't want people to survive the holidays.

The point is, as a child I preferred the safety of the pre-made, the regulated, the ready-bought.

I remember desperately wanting one of the pre-made cakes in the bakery for my birthday, but my Mum was an avid baker and would always make birthday cakes. Now, I wouldn't give a thought for a cake from a bakery, but I'd do anything for one of my Mum's - though I'm not sure how she'd cope with me being gluten-free.

I no longer find joy in the pre-made, the regulated, the replaceable. Don't get me wrong, I'm a sucker for a mass-market comfortable pair of pajama trousers from the Costco (and who doesn't love a good comfortable pair of shoes?) but I do genuinely find joy in the loop of a stitch or a brushstroke of paint, or frosting that is slightly wonky. It says a human was here and made this.

Mark's mother made us a quilt for our wedding and it still hangs proudly on the bedroom wall. I think it's absolutely perfect.

Mark's Mum could no doubt pick out where the thread was off-color or a stitch was wrong. Yet, that's part of what makes it ours. It's what makes it unique.

I like the flaws, the inaccuracies, the irregular. I like it in things and in people.

Now obviously, I'm not advocating that we all hand-make everything. You have to be realistic. I am clearly not a sock maker, and I'm probably not a steak pie maker either. Ask either of my kids about the time I decided I'd treat them by making a homemade steak pie. Even though that was years ago, it still gives them the dry heave.

But there's a difference between being realistic and plain old self-critical.

I had a bit of a fight with myself this week. Stuff that I planned to get done, I didn't. I was glutened by accident quite spectacularly and was out of it for a whole day. Then I got mad at myself for being so vulnerable that I literally could be taken out by one misplaced pie. Question: What kind of fucking idiot could be physically floored by a random piece of pastry? Answer: me. Talk about a flaw in the design.

But then in the middle of my post glutening, I put on my lovely new socks and I noticed the wee differences there are in the design, and I thought about my pal Anne and her Mum and how I love hand-crafted things. And then that made me think of my wee pal Michaelangelo - who I'm too young to have known personally despite what my kids might tell you.

Meaning and expression are found through the pursuit of perfect imperfection.

Who said I had to be perfect? Only me, when I'm being a complete arse. Everybody falls down sometimes and then they get up again. It's the flaw that makes us human.

Good old Michelangelo. We could have been pals. If I spoke Italian. If I was alive in the 16th century, and promised not to make him socks... or a steak pie.

COUNT TO 12

Time to consider

Here's the thing: I'm fine with change when it's on my terms. - when it's something like changing from having a hot tea in the afternoon, to having a nice cold drink because it's sunny outside.

But real proper change completely sucks, because there's a point where it's messy, and it feels like nothing can right itself again.

I'm moving offices this week and none of us are enjoying it. And yes I do have too much stuff and yes, I do hang on to too many papers and Mark can't understand why I have a stash of old letters and cards, but then again, I don't understand why he's got a box of old cables. To each his own, right?

And neither of the kids understand why we have boxes of old National Geographics and Mark and I both reply that they were in this house when we moved here and date back to 1937. But the kids don't care about that. They only care about them being stashed in boxes under their beds.

But even with the boxes under the beds bonanza, there are still tons of boxes everywhere.

My office is - or rather was - just one wee room in a small house that had a studio and bathroom. I don't really do in-person classes anymore, so I don't need the studio. Also, I'm heading off to do a bit of performing/showing off for much of the last part of this year, so I won't even be at a desk, let alone an office.

It all makes complete sense. Except...

I like to find stuff where I left it - mostly, and often especially, because where I leave stuff generally doesn't make sense to anybody else other than me. And I can't find anything. And everything feels lost. And yes, I know it's a first-world problem and I know that there are many people dealing with much much harsher challenges. But I really liked that office - a fact I was completely unaware of until now, when I don't have it anymore.

Now I've moved into my new office - which used to be Mark's. Mark is now ensconced somewhere behind the couch in the living room while we work out where to build an office pod in the backyard. Both the boys' beds are a couple of inches taller because of the amount of boxes under them - and Arthur who liked to come and nap in my old office and did his best to stay away from Mark's office, now wanders between both with a "What the Hell are you thinking?" expression, to which I reply "I don't know."

So I've been doing a lot of counting to 12.

When I was sick and genuinely had something real to complain about, a doctor friend told me that the body takes 12 weeks to properly adapt to anything. So, if you break a bone, it generally heals in around 12 weeks. With cancer, they check what the progress is generally every 12 weeks. 12 weeks is enough time for change to happen. So, after each procedure, I'd give myself 12 weeks to allow the recovery to happen, rather than stress about all the "could be's" along the way.

It worked so well for me then, I've carried on using the rule of 12.

When I really want to say something out of just plain annoyance, I count 12 seconds.

When I realize I need to stop for 5 minutes, I take 12 and properly reset.

I use 12 hours when I'm waiting for the answer for something, or when I need to make a big decision. For 12 hours I willfully do not stress, and amazingly after that wee break from obsessing, the answer usually comes to my mind fairly easily.

I'm using 12 days for times like now. Acknowledging and expecting 12 days of probable chaos, allows me to remember how small the issue really is. Even though when I look around everything might feel out of whack, it's not really. It will pass.

I use the 12-week rule all the time for work projects because writing can often feel a bit like chipping away at a mountain of rock with a teaspoon. But if you give yourself 12 weeks you will always have a clearer view of what is. It allows me to give myself time to learn.

I started writing this blog because I felt like I wanted to connect in some way outside of social media, but I was also worried about how vulnerable that might make me. Mark found me this Substack platform, and though I wasn't sure how to use it, I figured I'd hand it over to the 12-week rule.

On week 11, three different people pledged money for me to continue. I had no idea what that meant but apparently Substack had already suggested to readers how much they could pledge, and they did. I wanted to go round to those three peoples' houses personally and apologize for my unworthiness, and tell them the spoon and the cliff face analogy and thank them for their belief in me.

However, rather than bother them with my ridiculous neediness, I gave myself 12 weeks to develop and change. I collected the pledges and in doing so added a paywall. Then more people started paying and so I had to think of something that made it worth their while. I focussed on building stuff up - audio recording and doing little extra pieces.

I moved into this third set of 12 with an open mind about changing and developing while being mindful of consistency (Ooh, my mother would be proud of all my grown-up thoughts).

But in life, the unexpected is to be expected (so much so, that it should be called the completely expected in the first place). Over the past few days, several people have written complaining about the paywall and stating why I shouldn't do it because they can't afford to sign up for it, and I have felt completely shitty. I started writing Notes From The Valley as a way to connect. What happens when that connection is painful? None of this was meant to diminish anybody. But equally, I hadn't planned on being some sacrificial victim myself.

I took 12 hours to give myself time to consider. I moved more boxes and cleared a bit more space and organized what seemed to be a ridiculous amount of whiteboard pens. (somebody in this house seems to have a whiteboard pen problem.)

And, sitting amongst my own chaos, the answer became clear.

Each of us is in the middle of our own 12-week journey, and adulting can be rough.

I can't change the financial struggles or even the reasons behind the financial struggles that other people have. But I can completely keep my side of the street clean. Money does not define people. Thoughts and actions do.

I looked at the paywall and worked out how to change it to something I thought was more apt. Rather than the $80 Substack chose for me, it's now $52 because that's how many Sundays there are in a year. And I will carry on writing and some of it will be for free, and some of it won't, and some people will pay and some people won't, and that will be fine because we are all beautiful people doing the best we can.

I reminded myself of that as I let off a burst of expletives trying to lift the last box. On the top, it said, 'misc personal.' Why do I have to keep everything? It was so bloody heavy, I opened it.

At the top of the box was a fax (remember them?) from when I was in Australia in 1999. It was a cheeky Happy Birthday message sent from someone in London. Someone I know I'll never see again. It stopped me in my tracks.

None of this matters. None of it. We're all just here for a blip. Whatever immovable object we're facing, is not immovable because we're sitting on a planet rotating at 1000 miles an hour. Nothing is permanent. Nothing. Whether we like it or not, we all get to move forward.

If you're struggling right now, count to 12. Seconds, minutes, hours, days, weeks, or months. Whatever suits you best. Try it. It will probably turn out ok.

When you're going through change, nothing is normal and there comes a point where you doubt anything will feel normal again. But it does.

EGGS. DAD STYLE.

It's Father's Day here in the US this Sunday. Now I'm not one to reproach any chance for a wee celebration, but it seems to me these parent-celebrating Sundays - for all their best intentions - are basically a field day for a whole host of difficult emotions.

I completely loved my Dad, but I'm old enough to understand that not everybody had such a great time when it came down to either having parents, or being one. I reckon Mother's Day and Father's Day are a bit like bikinis: fine if you're lucky enough to have everything naturally in the right place, but otherwise a painful reminder that Nature doesn't always shape things perfectly.

And yes, I am grouchy. There's a weird weather thing going on in LA right now. It's dull and overcast and LA isn't built to be dull and overcast. It's built to be sunny. When the weather's weird in LA it feels like being in a theme park off-season: You can see there's fun to be had at some time but it's not happening now.

There's also the WGAW and SAG strikes, and the stuff in the news, and the constant nagging suspicion that this whole world is being run by complete imbeciles. In the stillness of the LA gloom, there's an ominous feeling. One way or another, something needs to give.

And I know I'm not alone in this, even the chickens are weird. In the middle of the week, Genghis the rooster was making the 'there's an emergency' noise at 5.30am. I opened the curtains and looked out the window. Once he saw me, he calmed right down and gave me an appreciative little dance. He just wanted to check in that everything really was ok.

With all the out-of-sorts-ness during the week, I decided there was nothing for it but to make Chinese Egg. This was one of my Dad's creations and is basically boiled egg with butter, toast, and salt in a cup. But boiled egg, butter, toast, and salt in a cup doesn't have a ring to it, so my Dad declared it was Chinese Egg instead.

It was the only thing my Dad could cook, and as a result it was what we ate when my Mum was away somewhere or if she was sick. So, even now I have it when things feel a bit out of place.

My Dad had a thing about eggs. A Second World War baby, he was convinced that if you had eggs in the fridge you were rich. Here in Tweddley Manor, we have chickens so we don't keep our eggs in the fridge. But it often does cross my mind that my Dad would think we had won the lottery by having fresh eggs on tap. I like to remind myself of that when I feel the world is out of whack.

I made some of my Dad's egg concoction for me and the kids, and we sat around the table laughing about how there's nothing particularly Chinese about it. My eldest did point out though, that he thought it was good that my Dad did credit the Chinese for something so tasty, when we live in a world where they keep getting blamed for everything.

I told them that though my Dad was almost a permanent West Coast of Scotland man, he did enjoy the idea of the exotic. Only the idea though. I made him a Thai chicken curry once, and even just looking at it turned his stomach. So not to hurt my feelings - and not to incur the wrath of my mother - he tried eating it. But he literally looked like a dog chewing a wasp. I will never forget the look of gratitude on his face when I said I had some breaded fish I could heat in the oven for him. Whenever I think I could have been a better daughter, I think of the Thai curry moment.

He was always a meat-and-potatoes guy, but as a fan of James Bond, he entertained the idea of being debonair. Once in a restaurant in Paris, and very enamored with the food (steak frites), he said with great benevolence to the waiter, "Muchos gracias." The waiter, momentarily confused, nodded politely and my father nodded back, signaling a bond of respect between them. Turning to see the bewildered expressions of everyone else at the table my Dad explained, "They like it when you talk foreign."

True, my Dad wasn't great on languages, but he could recognize a good guy in any nationality.

Over lunch, the boys talked about what to do for their Father's Day. Mark is notoriously difficult to buy a gift for, and there's only a certain amount of socks and underwear any human can own. Between us though, we

hatched a plan. And thus proved my Dad's philosophy -
The world always does looks better after Chinese egg.

My Dad was right about a lot of things. You don't need
to speak the same language to recognize a good guy,
and you don't need to be defined by titles either.

If you didn't have, or didn't get on with your father,
today can be about celebrating someone who offered
you guidance. If you struggle in a relationship with your
kids, offer up a bit of help to someone who needs a
hand.

If the day upsets you, ignore it. After all, just because
bikinis exist doesn't mean you have to wear one. And if
you really don't know how to feel, make some eggs.
And give them an exotic title. That always works.

WHERE THE WIND BLOWS

This week I taught a seminar for writers at Antioch University, Los Angeles. I know, catch me right? Next time you see me, you'll need to be calling me Ma'am.

The lecture is called "The Seriousness of Comedy - How and Why to Put Laughs in Your Drama." and is actually something I really do care about.

I like a joke, or at least a bit of light relief. I think there's always a place for humor.

In some of my darkest moments, there has been hilarity. I still smile thinking of a time when, just back from hospital post reconstructive surgery, wearing a giant muumuu (for that was all that would fit around my bruised and swollen body) I'd hobbled into the kitchen where my sister, Janice, was making tea. Out of the blue Cindy Lauper's 'Girls Just Want To Have Fun' popped up on Pandora.

Janice and I exchanged a look and a grin, and like giant land-locked synchronized- swimmers, we dropped into a dance that was as ungainly as it was hilarious. Sure there was shit to deal with, sure there was a ton of uncertainty, but you can't miss out on a dancing opportunity. Life can be a bit dramatic but there's nothing wrong with a bit of brightness between takes.

As Mark and the kids would no doubt tell you, I periodically sulk with the TV when there's yet another 'bleak' 'gritty' 'conspiracy' drama. Because honestly, over the past five years or so, I've had my fill of that in real life. Jeez, some days just looking at the news has been a white-knuckle ride.

And any new political dramas where the President might get kidnapped or The Prime Minister is in danger - uhm color me, I don't care. Now, I am not saying that the whole world of television should be nothing more than pleasant detective stories set in picturesque towns, where very gruesome murders happen but nobody's really that upset, and they still hold their annual bake sale. (Though obviously, I don't object to them.)

But I do think in terms of writing, you always have to look for a bit of brightness, because in my experience, misery can come knocking on your door without the need for an invitation. Joy sometimes needs a little more encouragement

Anyway, I was a bit nervous about the seminar, because although I am totally and utterly connected to the subject matter, it's been a long time since I was a college student myself. And times have changed.

Back in my day, everything was an 'in-person' experience. Fax machines were this crazy new invention we were all very excited about. We wrote with pens and paper. If you wanted to find something out, you had to get a book from the library. Now kids have every single piece of information they could ever want in a little device in the palm of their hands.

So, for all of my absolute belief in the content of the lecture, I could not help but come to the conclusion that in terms of college grooviness, I am an old fart. But that conclusion wasn't of any practical use. Old fart or not, they'd invited me to do a seminar. And I had agreed. And so a seminar must be done.

Then, it dawned on me that a while ago I'd conveniently had kids, and the eldest one is an actual college student. Result. So, I asked him what he expected from a lecture.

He considered. "Do you want an honest answer?' he said.

"Of course," I nodded, earnestly.

" Well, I always hope it will be interesting, but I generally accept I'll be bored," he said, nonchalantly.

This was news to me. "No," I said, surprised.

"Yeah. It's not that big a deal. It depends on whether it's something I'm interested in to start with, and also whether the lecturer is interested in being interesting. What about you? What would you expect from a lecture?"

I hadn't really thought about it before. "I dunno." I said.

Then I smiled, as my mind took me back to the days of pens and paper and new-fangled fax machines, and one particular lecture.

The lecturer I'm sure was a lovely woman in real life. In terms of lecturing though, she was tricky. She specialized in poetry and always gave off the air that she would rather be on some windswept hill writing verse in a notebook with a quill. She wore flowery gypsy skirts and lacy shawls and spoke of stanzas and couplets in the gentlest voice so that you literally had to strain to hear her.

For all her sweetness, I used to dread her classes. Either I was worried I was going to fall asleep, or I'd end up triggered with all sorts of prejudices and fears about how writing was no job for a real human, and I should give the whole thing up and try and get a job in the post office instead.

Then, during one lecture when we were drowning in the tedium of her whispering on about figurative language, rhyme and meter, she surprised the class by letting out a rip-roaring fart. It was spectacular. It was literally the kind of fart a rugby player after quaffing 7 pints of Guinness and a couple of Vindaloos would be proud of.

(Later students would talk about the fart being so loud, they saw her gypsy skirt billow with the force of it.)

There was a moment where none of us quite knew what to do. We sat motionless, partly through shock, but mostly trying to keep ourselves from laughing.

Then she smiled. A gentle, wistful smile, and said in her whispery voice. "I am so sorry about that. I must have had a bad pie at lunchtime."

That lecture I remember. That is the one that sticks in my mind.

I told Fergus. He thought it was funny, but not as funny as I still do. As funny as I probably always will.

"Lecturing is really just people saying stuff to other people." Ferg said, "And you always say to us that we should say what we mean. So just say stuff that you mean, and I'm sure you'll be fine."

So I did. And they were lovely. Hoorah for Antioch. And I didn't fart loudly. (But then I wasn't wearing a flowery gypsy skirt, so it wouldn't have been that funny if I had.) And neither did anyone else.

And I did say what I mean. And it was fine.

Misery is always easy to find. Joy often needs a little more encouragement. But it is always worth the effort.

INDEPENDENCE DAY

The angry mix

I have many faults but, thankfully, one of them is not using the phrase, "Let that sink in." Those four wee words linked together are some kind of kryptonite. They imply the writer is oh so much smarter than the reader, so for me they sound like nails scraping on glass.

Whenever I read a post with 'Let that sink in" in it, I have to sit on my hands to stop myself from commenting, "Are you a genuine condescending jerk or a regular person in disguise? #HowAboutYOUletthatSinkIn #AskingForAfriend"

But I don't. Mostly. Though this week I'm more tempted.

I am completely out of sorts this week. And a little explosive. But it's all the fault of the fireworks.

It's the fourth of July this Tuesday which means that for about the past fortnight, people (or as they're technically known -boneheads) have been letting off fireworks in the middle of the night. It's annoying for me, but it's completely terrifying for Arthur, who paces the rooms panting, or hides in a corner trembling.

My knee-jerk reaction is to wish a terrible life on those who let off fireworks at 3 o'clock in the morning. But in the blurry light of day, I remind myself that those who let off fireworks at 3 o'clock in the morning undoubtedly have a pretty shitty life to start with, otherwise they wouldn't find that sort of stuff entertaining.

Here in LA they even set them off during the daylight. The freakin daylight! Surely there can be no greater public declaration of stupidity. These idiots are probably the reason "let that sink in" was created in the first place.: Reminder. Socks go on before shoes. Let that sink.

Full-blown confession. I used to like fireworks. Loved them in fact. Bonfire night in London was always one of my favorites, and the giant fireworks display at Alexandra Palace was always a main event in the social calendar - by that I mean that we'd all go to the fireworks and then back to my house for baked potatoes and chili. (We're not talking fancy here.)

But that was in the old days when a public fireworks display was more than enough. And even if you did happen to buy fireworks, they were more phut phut fizz than full-on window-rattling explosion.

But since I moved to California, I've done a full 180. I'd go as far as saying I bloody hate them. They're pretty, of course they are. But they're ridiculously noisy and living in an area that gets so hot, it's in danger of going up in flames all on its own, they have to be right up there in completely stupidly, pointless ways to cause danger to people/animals/nature/property.

Our dog, Arthur, is a perky wee creature and it's horrible to see him tremble. And I know that currently all over town people are prepping to drug their perky wee creatures to help them make it through the next week without a heart attack. I could be out on a limb here, but I reckon if animals have to suffer in order for something to be deemed a party, then cancel the freakin' party.

You know what I always notice most about the 4th of July? The days after. When you take a walk on July 5th and the streets are eerily quiet. No birds singing. No wildlife. All sorts of creatures have either died or fled as a result of the actions of people who only know they're celebrating something by lighting a fuse.

If you happen to wander into social media you'll find all sorts of arguments about it. Angry-faced gits like me announcing that everyone should go to a public display and then leave that shit alone. And the pro-fireworks jerks arguing that even though it's illegal it's part of their freedom - to which I have to sit on my hands to stop myself commenting "Would this be the same freedom that veterans fought for on your behalf? #whythereAreNoFireworksOnVeteransDay #askingforAShellShockedFriend"

I always figured that freedom is the choice of how to behave - it's not that you get the right to remain unaccountable for that behavior.

For example: Whenever we stop at a traffic light and the driver in the next car has music blaring, and his window is down and inexplicably he has his hand dangling out of the window, I often have the urge to pull my window down and pull the guy's finger. But I don't. You know why? Because I am accountable. And also I don't want to get shot.

I feel like every single human I know is battling some kind of challenge. And that's not the stuff of lovely memes anymore. It's the truth. The pandemic kicked everybody's ass - whether they believed in it or not. The one reality even conspiracy nuts have to concede is that we have all been wounded by it.

We each of us have a fragility that wasn't there before and that fragility gives us the capacity to swing from being solid to vulnerable, hopeful to defeated, victim to douchebag. In truth, these people - or boneheads as they're technically known - are clawing for something. It is a desperate place to be if you can only connect to your own happiness by lighting the fuse. And I can navigate that when I get sleep, but I get so mad at stuff right now, I don't even like myself.

This Independence Day I need independence from my own head: Despite every window-rattling explosion convincing me people are assholes - I will remind myself most people really are fine.

And when the fireworks roar, goading me to believe that the world is going to ratshit, I can remind myself that it's not. In the midst of all the noise, a lot of really good people are consistently working to repair what is broken.

On July 5th when the streets are silent, and I feel such sorrow for the needless loss and suffering of actual living creatures we share the same planet with, I can take a breath and remind myself that I have a very privileged position. Not all living things get to make choices. I must keep in mind that I can, and aim to be accountable for those choices I make.

Yes this is an angry blog, but count yourself lucky. If I was one of those people who liked to use "let that sink in" this blog could have been a whole lot worse.

I think you know what I'm saying.

A LONG LONG WAY FROM CHRISTMAS

This has been what could be called an extreme week: Extreme highs and extreme lows. I was thinking of using some swanky metaphor about flying but as this was also the week that two friends I love dearly narrowly avoided being in a plane crash, I decided against it.

Mark and I are both a bit drunk-tired. If I tell you that just before sitting down to write this blog, I slept through the alarm and missed an important meeting, Mark found himself washing the dishes with hand soap, (I'm not sure how much the frying pan enjoyed it, but it sure as hell won't get acne) and I tried to make toast in the air- fryer, you get a rough idea.

The Valley has been exploding - at one point it seemed there was no end to the fireworks. Temperatures have been soaring, so the days were oppressively hot and, to add to the hassle, the day before Independence Day a neighbor who's not my flavor had a ridiculously noisy party. The police came to shut it down several times, but the neighbor - never a fan of the word no, when it refers to something he wants - only carried on having the party each time they left.

It went on till two or three o'clock in the morning apparently. I'm not exact on times as I was so whacked out, I fell asleep, but I have it on the authority of Fergus and his five friends who were visiting from out of state and had just returned from a gig.

So the next day when the neighbor appeared at the door with a bit of cake left over from the party and I refused it, he accused me of calling the cops (I didn't), then in a strange about turn, denied that the cops were even there (they were). Once we'd exhausted that little cycle, he claimed I was unneighborly (He might have been right about that. I wasn't feeling particularly neighborly) and announced as he flounced off with his cake that the next time I hold a party, he'll be the first person on the phone to the cops (I said I was fine with that).

My youngest had heard the whole thing from inside the house while hidden behind a 5-foot-tall lifelike figure of Santa Claus we'd bought from a friend kind of by mistake (like I say, it's been that kind of week).

We talked about a Reddit thing he'd discovered called 'Am I the Asshole." I said that I was on the fence about who the actual asshole was, and was completely open to the idea that it could be me, as I'm not great on very little sleep. But later that night when the same neighbor had a commercial-grade pyrotechnic display in his backyard, I conceded he was indeed 100%.

But honestly, it hasn't all been bad. Just really crazy. Like I say we - sort of by mistake - managed to buy a 5-foot Santa from a friend of ours who was moving home and needed him gone. His sudden appearance in the house was a source of great bemusement to Fergus's five friends from out of state, and confusion for Lachlan who had just returned from a class on Brazilian street fighting concluding that he's more a lover than a fighter.

Arthur who has been medicated to let him get through the fireworks fiasco has been adorably affectionate to all visitors and to the chickens. And it turns out the chickens don't give a toss about fireworks apparently, though they are still unreasonably judgemental of squirrels.

As am I.

We planted a sorry-looking little peach tree in the backyard a couple of years ago, and it has grown into a bit of a monster. This year it's laden with peaches, but it's a battle between me and one particularly feisty squirrel as to who gets to them first.

Earlier this week, as fireworks roared overhead, the squirrel and I eyed each other intensely before racing to get to the peach tree first. Mark, having witnessed it all, claimed it was like a scene from a bad Sylvester Stallone movie.

And Mark has had his own battles. He was worried about his beloved bees. The hive was getting full and the bees needed more space. He figured it was time to harvest some honey. So he did. Almost 20lbs of honey. From a big silver extractor machine shaped like a giant tin can, which was situated (conveniently) on top of a wooden box in the middle of the kitchen floor.

Like I say, this week has been extreme.

Last night we sat in front of the TV and watched Wycliffe - a very low-key UK detective drama from the 80s/90s where nothing much happens. It's our go-to when we've had a rough time because it's so relaxing to count how many bad sweaters there are. (Honestly, it's truly impressive).

There were fairly few fireworks, and no loud parties. The squirrels, the bees, and the chickens were asleep, and Arthur snored gently beside us.

"I'll have to go get jars for the honey tomorrow," Mark said.

I nodded. "Probably should also get a couple of hundred extra for several tonnes of peach jam too," I added.

"Yeah," he said.

"Crazy isn't it? All the time this noise was going on, the bees were just getting on with making honey and the peaches were quietly growing on the trees."

In the corner of the room, 5-foot Santa smiled a festive smile.

"Any thoughts on what to do with that guy?" Mark said.

"Probably shed," I said, "At least until it's some way close to December."

Mark nodded. 'Sounds good." and then laughed as a spectacularly bad sweater appeared on the TV screen. "That has to count for two," he said.

"Possibly three," I laughed.

Sometimes it feels a long long way till Christmas, but that doesn't mean there aren't still plenty of gifts to be found along the way.

THE TRUTH ABOUT VIKINGS

I've been thinking a lot about the Vikings this week, because what else is there to do when the temperature outside is heading for frickin' incinerator o'clock, other than think of Norse warriors who sailed cold and stormy seas?

You probably know this already, but disappointingly Vikings didn't really wear horned helmets. They were just bog-standard pudding bowl helmets, and the horned thing was supposedly the invention of 18th-century artists. (Curse you 18th-century artists and your, albeit well-meaning, complete fabrications.)

Also, Vikings weren't regularly putting their dead heroes on board an empty ship and sailing them off to Valhalla. Turns out the idea that Vikings put their dead heroes on empty ships, set fire to them and launching them into the water was mostly a story popularized by TV and movies. Apparently, Viking ships were too valuable to burn (that makes sense) and so sometimes they would bury heroes with their ships instead (which makes no sense.)

The burning ships not sailing off to Valhalla misinformation annoyed me more than the 'not really wearing horned helmets'. Because I've always pictured a burning longship sailing off on an empty sea as the perfect metaphor for accepting something you don't want to accept.

I met with a friend this week. He's a vibrant lovely witty person. Smart, sassy, and with a wicked sense of humor. But he struggles with memory loss.

He still makes me laugh. He still has the same twinkle. He still in one sentence can remind me why we're such friends. But each time we talk, he is a little less himself. His body is still here, but every time we meet, even that is a little less.

We often talk about the old times. I follow him when he takes me on a direction that makes no sense, and strive to answer each repeated question like it's the first time I've heard it asked.

I'm not great with it. I feel false. A fraud. Like I'm a bloody well-meaning 18th-century artist making shit up about Vikings wearing horned helmets, when clearly they never did at all.

But I remind myself I'm experienced at this. I'm an old entertainment mongrel and by its very nature, my business is based on pretense.

Those winter scenes in "It's a Wonderful Life" were filmed in the dead heat of Summer. Busby Berkley made his millions with heavily choreographed showgirls making kaleidoscopic displays, but in real life was a horribly messy drunk. And let's not even mention Bill Cosby.

Surely I too can pretend?

My friend and I are meeting because I'm gearing up to go out on the road with a show, so we won't see each other for a while. He is a little more frail than the last time and can't seem to focus like he used to. Sometimes he seems distracted trying to work out what he's doing here at all.

He used to always enjoy stories about the ridiculousness of entertainment and relish my capacity for a good Scottish moan. So I tell him that when you write a show, it's like a conversation I want to have. But when it comes to the time to sell your show it feels like you have to accost people and tell them that if they don't come and see it they'll be missing out. "And," I protest in my best indignant tone, "It frankly doesn't feel like you're giving people a gift if you have to keep punching them in the face to receive it."

There is a moment of confusion. A beat of doubt. Then he laughs loudly. Just like he used to, but not like he used to. Because in my ears, it's the sound of that moment of confusion that rings loudest.

I want to stop everything. I want to take his hand and say, "Can we stop this thing? Can this not be real? It's me, Lynn. Let's start again and we can go back to how things used to be."

But instead I laugh too. And we bask for a moment in the warm glow of friendship.

Sometimes it's not possible for the inside to match the outside. Sometimes all you really have is pretense.

Jeez, if I had a nickel for every person who'd droned on and on and on about what a wonderful partner they had, only to see them divorce the year after - well, let's just say I'd have a lot of nickels.

And how many times have my kids given me a scented candle for Christmas and I've told them it's the best scented candle I've ever had? Because it's never about the candle. It's about saying I love you and I always will.

So I look at him across the table and I smile. He hesitates just for a moment, then smiles back. He can see me. I am glad.

Soon I will be traveling. When I'm gone, my friend will be traveling too. One of us can return.

He loves me, I know it. And I in turn love him. On the inside I know who he is. Who to me, he will always always be.

But he has boarded the ship. There is nothing I can do but hold steady, as he sails. And I will keep my place on the shore, waving and smiling till long after he is out of sight.

He is a warrior. A beautiful, witty, brave, magnificent warrior. Valhalla will be lucky to welcome such a soul.

TRAVELING LIGHT

Adaptable Anoraks

I have an anorak. (I know, I can't believe I'm telling you this either). Anyway. I have an anorak that I've owned for more years than I care to remember - though I still think of it as new ...ish. Granted in The Valley there's not much need for a jacket most of the year, so anoraks don't get much wear. But I keep my anorak because it's useful. It can roll up into a wee ball to pack in a suitcase if need be, and emerge almost wrinkle-free to fend off any unexpected downpour.

I have a tendency to keep clothes. I don't think I'm miserly, but I'm specific. It's just that when I go to buy something, I find it's pretty much a variation on something I already have.

So I keep what I'm comfortable with, and get rid of things that look worn, or are not practical, or make me unhappy.

When I was a kid it was easy to work out when to get rid of stuff, because I grew out of it. But then I became an adult and I didn't change shape that much. Sure I get a bit fatter or thinner, and I got pregnant a couple of times, but I didn't ever grow six inches in height over the summer or have my feet suddenly change a couple of shoe sizes.

I remember when I was small, back in the old country, watching a TV show, and the posh lady presenting the show was talking about the great importance of a new stylish winter coat. She was very, very serious about it. A new winter coat was an absolute must for any self-respecting woman.

It made me worry about my mum, who I was pretty certain would not be getting a new winter coat - not with four kids to feed. What would happen to her? Would people gasp when she walked down the street? Whisper about her on the busses and shake their heads in sympathy? "Look at that poor woman. She appears to be wearing last year's Winter coat."

When I tearfully mentioned my concern to my Mum, she was remarkably unfazed - in fact, she smiled and said that she liked her current Winter coat, and there was 'always something.'

As I grew, I realized what she meant. It wasn't just winter coats but bikini bodies. Thanksgiving turkeys/ Christmas dinner/ Easter hams/ Mother's Day/ Father's Day/ Weddings/ Christenings/ Funerals/ Minimalism/ Maximalism/ How to modernize a bedroom/ Living room/ Kitchen, Hairstyles for the under 50s/ over 50s, Books you absolutely must read right now.

Because no matter what you do, there's a never-ending stream of how you could be doing it much better.

I'm helping Fergus to pack and I'm terrible at it. He's flying to Scotland tomorrow because he is working front of house at the Gilded Balloon during the Fringe, and visiting relatives beforehand. I have previews here in LA first, so I'll follow later.

Ferg is a California boy, and his answer to stuff is to take what seems sensible and to apologize, panic, and then find a solution if that turns out not to be enough. So when I remind him that in Edinburgh in August it's possible to have all four seasons in one day, he shrugs and tells me he's packed a couple of long-sleeved shirts and a jacket.

I look at his shirts and trousers, socks and pants, all tidily laid out for packing and it seems wrong. Where is the outfit he might need for mountain climbing/ scuba diving/formal dinners/ all sorts of random shit that he almost definitely won't need but should have just in case?

I worry he should pack more stuff. But when I point that out, Ferg says that in Scotland they have shops. And also washing machines.

And he is right.

Mark comes in to check that Ferg has all the travel adapters, chargers, and cables. Mark is a cable/ electronics packing guy who periodically bulk buys batteries. I used to say to him, "If there were a civil war and batteries became the currency, I do believe we would be the wealthiest people in this whole kingdom." Since 2020 I don't say shit like that anymore.

"Travel adapter?" says Mark.

"Yep," says Ferg.

"Currency in cash in case you can't use your card?"

Ferg checks his wallet and nods. "Uh huh."

Tickets? Passport?

"Yup. And yup."

I try to think of something to ask him that he might not have, but there's nothing I can think of.

Later that night I confess to Mark that I'm convinced there's something I've forgotten.

"You are always like that," he says, "It's your not-enoughness. You get it when you've something on your mind."

I was about to deny it. And then thought about the day before when I'd seen a client, made six jars of peach jam, froze another three pounds of peach slices (the peach tree in the backyard is a rampant overachiever), finished a written treatment, made dinner for me, Mark and the boys, did two lots of laundry, and yet still sat down at the end of the night and said, "I feel I've not done much today." And Mark, who had been fitting new batteries into the remote control at the time, had snorted and said, "Is something bothering you?"

And a little too quickly I had replied, "No."

God dammit, he was right. My not-enoughness. It is me. Older than my anorak and twice as familiar. The nagging feeling that I've somehow not got it right, and that somebody somewhere has secretly got the whole answer to every part of life sorted. And that person is definitely not me. So I need to work harder, stress, think, and do stuff to make everyone around me safe.

I get it when there's something else bothering me. And it's stupid because safety is never a given and not the same as stagnation. And life is for living anyway. And no matter how well prepared you are, stuff happens, and being alive is all about the stuff happening. That is how we learn.

And there it was. The thing I'd been forgetting. The most important thing - To tell Fergus not to sweat about the small things, because there's "always something."

Also that although he's a proper grown-up, I am his big daft mother. So I will always worry, even though he's completely capable. And I love him. And I'm proud. And I want him to have his adventure.

So I told him. And he laughed and he hugged me, and he showed me that he'd packed his anorak and reminded me to pack mine. Cheeky bugger!

It's been a long time since I physically grew out of something, but I have now. Screw you, not-enoughness, and also screw you posh lady on the telly from around 50 years ago.

It's fricking roasting outside and so I don't need a new winter coat. Not now and perhaps never. Let people whisper on the bus. Let them shake their heads at me in sympathy. Let them claim I'm not a self-respecting woman.

And when it does rain as one day, it inevitably will. I will be absolutely fine in my new..ish old anorak

SHIFTING ATOMS

Everyone's favorite Roman

If I had to pick out my favorite ancient Roman (and who hasn't done that?) it would have to be Titus Lucretius Carus, or Lucretius as he's known to his pals.

Now you might have thought I'd have chosen Elagabalus for comedy purposes. Generally considered the most embarrassingly bad Roman Emperor there ever was, Elagabalus proved that just as a broken clock tells the right time twice a day, even a complete imbecile can bring something useful to the world, by inventing the whoopee cushion. (In a similar fashion that's how the UK got the Boris bike.)

But no. My favorite ancient Roman is Lucretius, because he was so eloquent and smart. He's a poet (but don't hold that against him) and in his work, The Nature Of Things, he states,

"We are each of us angels with only one wing, and we can only fly by embracing each other."

I like that. I think it's the clearest depiction of what life is ever.

It's been a strange old week. Everything is on the move: Ferg is now happily ensconced 5000 miles away. Mark and Lachlan and I have been fighting off some lurgy. I opened Storyland in LA, and am getting ready to head 5000 miles to meet Fergus.

Lachlan keeps asking when I'm going - not because he's worried about it (though there's a little part of that) but because in the house turnaround, we've decided to swap his bedroom with Mark's office. This means there's a whole load of stuff to move from one side of the house to the other, and it's been universally agreed, that this would be better happening when I'm not physically here.

He's very much looking forward to moving into 'the apartment' - so-called because his soon-to-be room has its own bathroom, is connected to the laundry room, and has a separate entrance to the kitchen. He's happy because he feels it gives him more independence. I'm happy because it's about as much independence as I want my 16-year-old to have. And Mark's happy because he hated that office. It's a weird shape for a desk and will be much better with a bed and all Lachlan's stuff.

It's good. It's all progress. But I am a little on the melancholy side.

It's my mother's birthday on Thursday and though she's been gone almost 15 years it doesn't feel that long ago at all. I can hear her opinions on everything that's going on. I know how thrilled she'd be about Fergus, how concerned she'd be about the show: "So, how did it go? When are you bringing it to Cumbernauld" and how much she'd laugh about the machinations of the magnificent force of nature that is Lachlan. She'd worry that I wasn't eating properly/ getting enough rest/ taking care of myself. She'd remind me that everybody always feels better after a haircut.

I hear her in my head like she's here. I consider what she'd think about something when I'm thinking about something. And I'm good.

And then along comes something like a birthday and I remember that she died, and I miss her all over again.

Over 2000 years ago, my wee Roman pal Lucretius talked about the Universe. He said it was made of an infinite amount of atoms (I know. I'd thought atoms were a modern thing too). He said that they're small but not infinitely small. And that they're strong in everlasting singleness. That they're impenetrably hard. Indivisible. Unalterable. Eternal.

He said that all things were made of these atoms, and that when a person dies, their atoms would disperse and then make something else. These atoms will always remain contained in the Universe. They may move around but they do not leave. Like the stuff from Lachlan's bedroom moving to Mark's office and vice versa. Everything still exists but in a completely different space and form.

I miss my Mum. Of course I do. I miss her laugh. I miss how it felt to cuddle her when I was small and she was grown, and when I was fully grown and she got small. I miss arguing with her over her weird philosophies, like how cream cakes weren't bad for you and Rock Hudson really did like women.

But as my best wee ancient Roman pal, Lucretius would remind me, she is still here. Indivisible. Eternal. In everlasting singleness. Embracing me. Helping me to fly.

Happy Birthday, Mum.

LONG-HAIRED LOVER FROM LIVERPOOL

I had a whole story for myself when I was a kid about the way things were going to be, and hardly any of it has worked out that way. Although if things had worked out the way I planned when I was a kid, I would nowadays be known for heating pies and be referred to as Mrs. Jimmy Osmond.

The first thing I ever remember writing was a poem about Jimmy. A newspaper in Scotland called The Evening Times was holding a competition - the prize was a life-size cardboard cutout of Little Jimmy Osmond. (Who at that point in time was admittedly only about 4' 5"). To win, entrants had to write something interesting or draw a picture of Jimmy. I've always been dodgy with the illustrating so I wrote a poem instead. It went like this:

> *For Jimmy O.*
>
> *He's great, he's fab, he's number one*
>
> *He's Mrs. Osmond's youngest son.*

That's it.

Unsurprisingly I didn't win, but I was cool with that, because I had other plans. Ever since seeing him on Top of the Pops at Christmas, singing his number 1 hit, 'Long Haired Lover From Liverpool', 7-and-a-half-year-old me had decided on marrying him - not making do with a cardboard cutout.

My strategy at the time was not that complicated. I just repeated that I was going to marry Jimmy Osmond over and over again with the conviction that just repeating the same sentence over and over again means that makes it true (Basically an early form of Trumpism - though in my defense I was 7 and a half and not a grown-assed man.)

The way I saw it, Jimmy and I were to spend our weekends at our very own caravan in Arbroath, and on weekdays we'd travel between Cumbernauld and America. Jimmy was too short to drive so we'd have a chauffeur-driven Vauxhall Victor. At night we'd dine on such luxuries as roast potatoes and Fray Bentos pies. All vegetables would be banned. (apart from potatoes obviously and peas which were ok.)

Sometimes I'd lie awake at night thinking of the house we would have: I figured we'd have to have an actual dining hall to be able to feed all of the Osmonds and all of the Fergusons at the same time. And that the hall and the dining table should be purple. I'd calculate how many family-sized Fray Bentos steak pies we'd need to feed everybody, and speculate whether we should get new-fangled, double-glazing for all the windows to help drown out the sound of all the girls screaming for Donny.

I figured we'd adopt children as I planned on being a mother but I wasn't going to go through any of that 'taking off clothes' nonsense with boys in order to get them. (I absolutely knew Jimmy would understand.) And we'd get a dog. And some more guinea pigs.

Almost half a century later, I am happy to report that thankfully repeating something over and over again doesn't make it true. Jimmy and I never got married, which was undoubtedly for the best.

And it's been a long long time since I've imagined any sort of life as Mrs Jimmy Osmond, though I do still occasionally find myself lying awake making up stories. Because I'm traveling to Scotland tomorrow, mostly my head is full of lists.

What if the flight is canceled? What if I miss the connection? How long will I be jet lagged for? How easy will the tech rehearsal be? When will I get settled in digs? Are the posters out? Are the leaflets out? Will people come?

Lists and lists and lists. Of a whole load of stuff I have at this point absolutely no control over - especially at 3 o'clock in the morning.

Last night, completely out of the blue, my mind wandered over to Jimmy, and I smiled a giant Osmond-sized smile.

10 year old me had no concept of computers or the notion of living abroad. I couldn't imagine anybody would actually want my opinion about anything, or that I'd ever be able to survive the death of my Guinea Pig whenever that happened.

I had definite plans for how I wanted my life to be, but my vision was limited by my then experience.

If my life had turned out exactly as 10-year-old me had had my heart set on, it would be pretty horrific. Similarly, if my life continually turns out exactly as I plan it to be, it will be equally kind of disappointing.

What makes life interesting is the unknown. What gives life energy is facing challenges. Getting what you need is not always the same as what you believe you want.

Though it can be impossible to believe it at the time, you really can grow to enjoy vegetables other than potatoes and peas. You really do survive the death of your guinea pig. And that thing of taking off clothes with boys is not all that bad.

Life is experiential, not a row of tick boxes. As much as I might eternally want it planned out, life arrives on life's terms and I'll have a much better time if I go with it.

I considered if The Evening Times were to run a competition for a life-sized cardboard cutout of Jimmy Osmond nowadays, I might write something like this:

Dear Jimmy.

Thank you for your bad sweaters, your smiley smiliness and your terrible Christmas number 1. Thank you for never being my long-haired lover from Liverpool (via Utah) but turning out to be an inspiration anyway.

Yours sincerely,

Not your Sunshine Lady from LA (via Cumbernauld) Lynn

*****

Obviously I wouldn't win, and that would be a good thing. Though a life-size cardboard cutout of Jimmy Osmond could keep Mr Tweddle company while I'm gone.

Scotland, I am coming for you, and I'm so looking forward to the ride.

FIND YOUR LIGHT

So, my solo show Storyland opens at The Gilded Balloon tomorrow, and today - like the day before any show opens - the same story runs through my mind.

Back in the day when dinosaurs roamed the earth, and I was at drama college, I was lucky/unlucky/coerced enough to take part in our second-year stage spectacular – a theatrical version of the epic Victorian novel, 'Vanity Fair.' If you don't know anything about Vanity Fair the novel, it follows the lives of Becky Sharp and her pal, Emmy, during and after the Napoleonic wars.

Because the story is set in pretty society homes, where pretty girls with bouncing curls wonder whether their soldier loves them, and because I am – and always have been – an uncurly Scottish person who is as much at home in Victorian society houses as I would be amongst a reclusive tribe in the Amazon jungle, I was cast as a narrator. My job was to stand at the side of the stage and introduce each scene as it was about to be acted out.

The director was very ambitious. There was a variety of sound and lighting effects. The play was double cast, which meant that there were twice as many people learning the same play, and they would alternate each night.
It took place in an old-style theatre where the stage is

182

raked – which means it's on a slope to make better sight lines for the audience.

The set was fairly simple, a cluster of little platforms on wheels that could be constructed into different setups - though you don't have to be an engineering genius to work out that when you have a stage that is effectively a little hill, wheeled anythings are asking for trouble.

Rehearsals were tense. But I know what you're thinking, it would all work out right in the end, right? Wrong. Very very wrong.

The over-ambitious lighting design was impossible for the lighting operators (also students) to master. This meant that during the actual performances, lights would switch on and then suddenly switch off again.

Sometimes the stage would remain in darkness for what seemed like half an hour. Other times the light would appear, randomly, somewhere else.

An actor might make a dramatic entrance in full light, and start his great speech, only for the light to suddenly disappear.

Then, the light would frenetically reappear on an empty piece of stage, or another actor, or on the audience, or occasionally on a tech trying to silently set up another part of the stage for the next scene. And the actor would yell their speech, part theatrically/part distress-call into the darkness.

Even after all these years, I still laugh when I remember the lights going out on one actress during a particularly emotive speech. The light then reappeared, full beam, on a tech girl called Lesley – looking terrified and not at all curly or Victorian – holding a side table in one hand and half a roast chicken in the other.

But the lights weren't the only problem. There was still the issue of those platforms on wheels on the sloped stage.

One particular actor would invariably jump onto the little platform to proclaim something of great importance, only for the little platform to then roll at significant speed towards the orchestra pit.

Sometimes the lights would go off simultaneously. And all you could hear in the darkness was the sound of the wheels and an actor whispering, "Fuck.Fuck.Fuck.Fuck. Not again. Fuck.Fuck.Fuck." under his breath, culminating in either a bang and a yelp, or the sound of the wheels screeching to a halt and a sigh of relief.

Throughout it all, because of my sheer un-Victorian uncurliness, I stood at the side of the stage and tried my best to explain to the audience what part of the story we were at.

Sometimes I was in light. Sometimes I wasn't. Sometimes I was part of a play. Sometimes it was more of a rescue mission.

When I left college and meandered into stand-up, periodically I'd work at places that were considered pretty tough: like the club in South London where the bouncers ended up being jailed for manslaughter, or the club in Northern Ireland where they informed me that they'd only had one woman play there before, and she'd escaped out the back door before the show ended, or hosting the ridiculously rowdy Late N Live in the Edinburgh Fringe.

Before going on, I'd stand at the side of the stage and look out into the bear pit of the audience. I'd think to myself, as long as there was a working light and the stage wasn't on wheels, then the odds of everything working out fine were even.

And mostly, they were.

And on the times they weren't, Vanity Fair taught me that even the shittiest shit-show will one day exist only in stress nightmares, or in stories told to friends.

So wherever you are today – whether it be pre, mid, or post shit-show, know that whatever bothers you will one day just be a crazy story you tell.

And tomorrow's first show will bring what it may. All I can do is look for the light.

Aug 20, 2023

ONE STEP AWAY

The first thing you need to know about Edinburgh is the stairs. Nothing is flat. Everything is a hill or a stair.

When we visited when the kids were small, my youngest announced outraged as we were heading up the hill to the castle, "Who put this big slope here? It's not convenient!"

But the hills and steps are not just geographic. They're also a complete metaphor for the Edinburgh Fringe. Some days you're climbing up, other days you're heading down. Expect the road to be bumpy.

I've been here before many times, and though I generally forget about how to pack properly for Edinburgh (Anorak and comfy shoes essential) I always come with my head prepared.

My method of dealing with the Fringe is generally to keep a step back. I live on my own slightly away from where the action is. If I don't have written work to do, I spend the time before the show pottering about Edinburgh's pretty wee streets, or if it's not raining, sitting on a park bench enjoying (what once wasn't, but now is) a foreign climate.

After shows, I'll have a drink with mates and then head back to digs for client sessions courtesy of Zoom, and to talk to Mark and Lachlan who are still in LA.

I know it's not very rock n roll, but it's a system that works.

As a result I'm always a step away from the action, and periodically feel like Edinburgh is doing a show for me, rather than the other way round.

It was like that one day last week, a day I called, "The Three Sisters"

Sister 1 was the supervisor in the refectory. I live in posh student accommodation (if there is such a thing) on a campus. In the mornings they serve a hot breakfast in the on-site refectory. It's busy and fast, but they had me at unlimited cups of tea. One of the staff was having a meltdown about something (she seemed like a professional complainer) then moved back in indignant umbrage, knocking my arm and pouring scalding hot liquid over my hand. As dramatic as that might sound, I'm the mother of two kids and have therefore burnt my hand plenty of times before. It wasn't serious, but it could have been if it had been a child or a frail person. I made it clear to the complaining woman, that generally when it comes to performance it's best not to do it next to boiling liquid and other people. Then I headed off to have breakfast, considering the matter sorted. But the Supervisor followed me. She was concerned. She wanted to know if I needed anything. A cool pack, anything. I reassured her that as I was a big leathery-skinned person I was fine, and as we talked I realized she wasn't ok. "Are you alright?" I asked. She replied - way way too quickly - that she was. So I did what my kids call, 'prodding eyes', which makes people fess up.

I said as a potential burns victim, I needed her to sit with me and have a cup of tea (of course I had two - tea is unlimited) and her story poured out. I can't tell you what it was, because that is her story, but at the end we had a cuddle and I told her that she couldn't be accountable for other people's bad behavior. She could only lean into what she knew to be right, accept that she was doing her best, and let others face the consequences of their own decisions.

And she left and I ate breakfast, I thought about how I'd learned that lesson many moons ago at the Fringe.

Sister 2 was also at the digs. I was in my room, and there was the obligatory knock on the door and "Housekeeping".

I opened the door to a wee woman with a cart full of towels and the like. She looked fucking exhausted. "Are you alright?" I asked. "Oh yes, uh huh," she replied with polite efficiency. And I know I shouldn't have, but I'd already had my prodding eyes out that day, so they just kind of happened. "Are you sure?"

Her face crumpled. "I have so many rooms and I just don't know how to get them all done." And she explained the rest of her story, which is again hers. Anyway, I told her I was staying for a while and I'm an introvert so she'd be doing me a favor if she didn't do my room every day. Periodically I said I'd come and nudge her for clean linen, and we could arrange a time for a wee hoover here and there, but otherwise, we were good. She smiled and thanked me and I closed the door.

There was a knock on the door 5 minutes later. It was my new wee pal from housekeeping, bringing me some extra cups and of course more tea. I was thrilled.

I closed the door thinking about another lesson I'd learned at the Fringe: Friendship and compassion make the overwhelming feel much more manageable.

Sister 3 was on the bus home after the show (rock n roll eh?) And to be honest, I should have known. The bus was busy and there was only one empty seat next to a tiny wee lady with a wheeled walker. It was so convenient, it was conspicuous in its emptiness. But I was tired after the show and carrying a heavy bag. I had barely placed one butt cheek on the seat when she started yelling about how her walker didn't have brakes and I was putting my life in my hands. She demonstrated the danger by ramming the walker into my legs.

"Lady, cut that out!" I said in no uncertain terms.

"You can't sit here!" She yelled.

I turned, giving her what my kids call angry eyes, and said. "I am sitting here. It's only a couple of stops and this is where I am sitting. Get over yourself. Understand?"

She gulped. And was silent. There was such an air of relief on the bus, I almost expected a round of applause.

I had earned her respect. After a moment, she leaned in and conspiratorially whispered, "I can tell you the best busses to get Covid on if you want?"

"No thanks, I'm good," I replied.

"Have you had Covid? Anybody here have Covid!!!!?" she yelled

The woman in the chair alongside me scowled. A man diagonally in front tutted. And I found myself starting to giggle.

"You know," my new traveling companion explained, "You can get Covid 2500 times?"

I nodded, keeping my mouth shut. It was wrong, but I really wanted to laugh.

"So, " she said, "How many times have you had COVID?"

"2499 times" I replied, cheerfully.

She looked at me like I had just explained some theory of quantum physics and nodded knowingly.

I laughed about talking with the wee lady all the way home. Another Fringe lesson: when faced with craziness, sometimes the best thing is to laugh with it and enjoy the ride.

Back at the digs later, I talked with Mark on Zoom. We talked chickens, and bees, and life. Then Lachlan came on the call and talked about his first day back at school. Then they asked me how Edinburgh was going.

"Oh you know," I said, "Edinburgh is ups and downs. Nothing is flat."

And Lachlan laughed knowingly "Yeah, I can't believe they put that slope there. It's very inconvenient"

REAL GOOD TIMES.

Not all portable timing devices are the same. You can get your digital timers and of course little mechanical ones, or you can use the timer on your phone. But timing stuff on your phone can look rude and though digital ones are definitely better, mechanical ones are a lot easier to find when trawling the aisles of bargain shops in Edinburgh.

This information is good to know when you have a chicken in the oven or you're doing a stand-up set.

I know there's a story that stand-up is the hardest job in the world, but anyone who's stood for even 5 minutes at a microphone telling jokes will tell you that's rubbish. Yes sometimes it can be a bit grueling, or a bit boisterous, sometimes your ego can take a wee bit of bruising, but for the most part it's like a good stretch.

There's no illusions with stand-up. If people like your work, they laugh. If they don't, they won't. Maybe more jobs should be like that - it might make tax offices more pleasant, though political debates would be even more miserable.

I gave myself a wee gift this week and went off to do a wee bit of stand-up. I like to do that when I'm out on a run of some other show, as it's the most brilliant way to blow off the cobwebs. So when my good friend Viv messaged me back in June about doing a gig in August, it was no decision at all to say yes.

The Edinburgh Fringe is amazing but it messes with everyone's mental health. With literally thousands of shows going on around you every hour of every day, it's hard not to get caught up in other people's challenges.

As I headed to the gig I was feeling particularly dark. Too many old colleagues of mine are really struggling with proper issues. I hate that though you can wish the very best for someone, Fate can have different ideas.

But as soon as I walked in the door to the gig, my mood lifted. I'm not suggesting it was like coming home, because I don't have fifty punters huddling round a bar in my living room, but it felt so comfortably familiar, I could feel everything relax.

The gig had already started and had just reached the first interval when I arrived. As I went to the bar, two ladies, were giggling and smiling. "You don't remember us do you?" one said.

I smiled trying to register. I hate being rude but I really had no idea.

"Don't be daft," said the other. "Of course she won't remember" Then she turned to me and smiling sweetly, said, " We came to a gig of yours 20 years ago and we'd just dropped acid." "Oh," I said, not really sure what else I should be saying.

When I headed into the room, I was greeted like an old friend. Though I hadn't met these comics before other than online, there is generally a great camaraderie between stand-ups. Yes, there is the occasional nutter, or some overblown ego with feet, but for the most part, we generally recognize each other as part of the same tribe.

Des the compere told me that a great deal of the audience were Latvians.

"Oh," I said again.

I maybe wasn't feeling quite as relaxed now. Acid-dropping ladies and Latvians is an unusual mix. But in stand-up, you must go with the flow. I looked over the crowd and saw a face I recognized. A lovely lovely friend I know because she used to be married to my old dentist.

It certainly was shaping up to be a fairly surreal night.

I stood at the back watching two very different acts do brilliantly, then there was another interval and then it would be me.

I was booked to do a 20-minute set - or longer if I wanted to. When you're closing the show, you pretty much have free reign. But too many years of compereing have unwittingly made me an absolute stickler for time. I don't settle with free reign. Hence the timer.

Before I start a set I always start a timer telling the audience I have a chicken in the oven. Or a pie. Or a lasagna. Sometimes a quiche -something that has to be attended to that means I only have a set time. When the timer goes off, I leave, even if I'm in the middle of a punchline. I don't know whether audiences enjoy the audacity or just knowing that I will leave no matter what, but it generally makes the process smooth, and then - unburdened by time constraints - I can open up my set and just play.

But the only timer I could find here was mechanical. And a bit too ticky. I had a negotiation with the audience about the noise of it when I started and most people decided it was just fine apart from one guy near the timer. We agreed he could put his hat over it to cover the ticking. After a couple of minutes he put his jacket over it as well.

And we laughed and I talked. And I talked. And we laughed. And it was lovely. Latvians really are lovely people. As are acid-dropping lesbians. As is my friend who used to be married to my old dentist. But after a while I felt I had been talking for a very long time.

I took my very loud timer out from under the hat and coat and it read 4 minutes. I couldn't believe it. It was still bloody ticking but it was useless. I checked with Des, the compere, and apparently I'd been on 35 minutes. The audience assured me I could stay but I informed them it would be irresponsible to ruin a lovely roast chicken, and I headed offstage into a flurry of cuddles and laughing while Des closed up the show.

But by then we'd all decided we liked each other so led by the Latvians, a group of us returned to the stage and sang songs celebrating Latvia. It was joyous.

They sang with great passion, while the acid-taking lesbians, and the lovely friend who was married to my old dentist, the comics, Des and me sang with less tuneful enthusiasm.

And at the end, I presented the guy with the hat and the jacket with my mechanical timer. He received it like I'd given him the nobel prize.

Later as I headed home, I felt lighter, better. Yes time passes. Of course it does. Sometimes way faster than you think. Sometimes painfully fast. And yes nothing and nobody are forever. And yes, sometimes too easy to yearn for the past.

But joy is to be found in the weirdest of places, with people you might not even have met yet. Memories may be precious and bittersweet, but they shouldn't get in the way of making many new memories.

Life is less predictable than a dodgy digital timer.

When you find joy, seize it. Embrace it. Enjoy it like a warm bath. And maybe make a plan to visit Latvia.

BIG SMALL WORLD

Fergus flew back to LA this week, while I continue on the tour. It was hard to see him go. I know he's heading home. I'm perfectly aware I'll see him in a few weeks. But there are some feelings over which we have no power. They belong in the realm of instinct rather than thought, and will not be quieted by reason. He's still my son, even though he's a grown-up man. Wherever he is, a part of me will forever be also - even when that's 12 and a half hours of him being 70000 feet in the air and inconvenient as shit.

I'm never good with him flying. I'm unsettled when he's in the air. I like him to be one place or the other. I like things to be clear.

The night before he left, we stood in the backyard of my sister's house, looking up at a moon that seemed so close you could touch it.

It has been wonderful spending time at my sister's. In between working in Edinburgh, we retreat here, for hot meals and cozy beds and family. Fergus loves his Aunty Janice and Uncle Eddie. He barely remembers my parents as he was so young when they passed, so Janice and Eddie represent more than just an aunt and uncle. Sometimes Janice and I will talk about the old days when we were in our early 20s. Ferg likes to hear stories about what has gone before.

Standing in the backyard, we couldn't help but marvel at the size of the moon. How clear it was. It felt like a change of energy was in the air. The season is changing. Time, like everything else, is not ours to control.

"Are you looking forward to going home?" I asked.

"I am," he smiled. "Though there will be plenty I miss. Sausage Rolls, Greg's the Bakers, Uncle Eddie and Auntie Janice."

Janice and I laugh and all three of us have a cuddle. And we are for a single moment under the big smiley moon, reminded how precious life is.

I'm not really one for astrology - I'm not against it, but I know so little about it that it feels general to me. I suspect real astrology is more like mathematics than it is like a wee generic paragraph on a list somewhere dedicated to people who share your birth month. But of late there's definitely something going on with the planets. Literally everyone I talked to this week was dealing with trying to move the immovable. Something that should be a simple fix inexplicably was not, and the more people struggled, the more stubborn the task became. Despite any effort, the clear remained resolutely unclear.

Of course my feeling might be less to do with the planets and more to do with an old washing machine.

Mark and I (as old hippies) both hate needless landfill, and as Mark is brilliant with any kind of anything that has working parts, he will generally look to see if something can be fixed before it's replaced. Hence why Mark decided to fix the washing machine. But the washing machine has become the Moby Dick to his Captain Ahab, working one day only to be defiantly broken the next day when fixed back in place.

Navigating the time difference we talk about it over the phone. Victory one day, and defeat the next. And yet the battle continues.

Like the rest of the world, Mark and I exist in 24-hour time spans. But for the moment our time spans have an 8-hour time delay. There is a distance between us, both of geography and of time. What I may tell him is an unsurmountable problem in one phone call is fixed by the time of the next. What he sees as a problem in one conversation is solved by the next - apart from the washing machine that is.

A sleepless night before Fergus flew was followed by a restless night waiting for news that he'd landed.

In the morning. A text came from Mark:

"Picked Ferg up from the airport. He's fine, fed, showered and tucked up in bed. Everything's good, though I'm thinking it's time for a new washing machine. Love you x"

That night I started the tour. The first show was lovely.

And on the drive back afterward, the moon behind the clouds shone down.

A TRIP ON THE TRAIN

For the first time since I arrived in Scotland, this week I had the chance to take a wee break to the seaside. It's ridiculous that in a country pretty much surrounded by water, it's taken me this long. But work is work and I come from a long line of 'First things first people': Get your head down and focus on what needs to be put in place. Once that feels steady, take some time to rest, to lift your head up and have a look around.

So, day off in hand, I took a train to Gourock on the West Coast to meet up with Mark's parents for lunch and then a good friend from college late afternoon.

I grew up using public transport and I like it. It's something I miss back in LA. Everything is too much about cars. Here in Scotland, the trains for the most part are magic, the bus service is frequent and there's even a wee underground in Glasgow if you fancy traveling around and around.

Mark and I have agreed that at some point we'll take a trip together on the Orient Express, but for now with me in Scotland and Mark back in the Valley, a wee trip to the coast on Scotrail feels like a very close second.

The fact is there is nothing better than sitting on a half-empty train, cup of hot tea in hand, and having the time to just look out the window at the world going by.

Last week when I was starting the tour, those cows in that field were no doubt in that same field, maybe even in the same arrangement they are now. That half-constructed bungalow we pass along the way, slightly less constructed when I landed in August. Toys strewn around gardens were probably in the hands of kids yesterday who are now sitting behind desks at school. Because there's a whole world happening, when I have my head down. While I focus on my 'first things first' the rest of the world has their own firsts too.

There's such an understated beauty in the West Coast. It has a past that is both industrial and vacational. On the same small coastline where great ships were built, The Queen Mary and The Queen Elizabeth, my family and many others would spend two weeks in the Summer when we were kids, paddling in shallow waters, studying rockpools, out in little rowboats mackerel fishing.

The train stops at a town where Mark grew up, and journeyed from being a toddler taking his first steps, to being a teenager stepping out into the world. Years when I never knew him. Years I had no idea of his existence though he lived within 30 miles of me.

I'm on the verge of being overwhelmed by the magic of it all when I'm distracted by the smell of cooked bacon. A big guy who's dressed as a great homage to khaki has seated himself at the table across the aisle.

As the train leaves the station, he unwraps some combo of cooked breakfast. He doesn't notice me. He doesn't notice anyone. He is entirely focused on his prey of buttered rolls with bacon and a diet Coke.

I find myself wondering where he's going, and where he's been, and wondering how he manages to navigate such a wealth of saliva.

I am grateful that I have only 7 minutes of getting to hear the functionality of his digestive tract before the train pulls into Gourock. As soon as I step off onto the platform, the smell of bacon is replaced by the smell of the sea. It takes me back 50 years to visions of me on the beach with a bucket and spade and my Dad.

Mark's parents are there to pick me up. Mark's Mum has planned ahead and is very careful to make sure we eat at somewhere gluten-free and I am thrilled by the presentation of fish and chips. We have a lovely time talking and pottering around the shops. It's so calm and easy and I catch my breath when I consider that because these two people met and fell in love, they gave birth to a human who is the foundation of my whole world. Incredible really.

I consider how sometimes I'm so busy being on my own journey that I forget how amazing other people's journeys are too. It's so good to take a day off.

After meeting up with Mark's parents, I go to hang out with Lou and Alec. Lou and I were at college together years ago, but talk like we just hung out yesterday. Alec was at school with Lou. They went off and had separate lives and then came back together again. We each of us have been in a billion different places and yet sit around the table in this beautiful little gallery talking easily with all we have in common. I feel lucky.

We sit and drink a wine called Ned and eat delicious cheese called Fat Cow and the names make us laugh freely, as does the ridiculousness of life and chance and the stories from the old days.

Their gallery is called Crow Cottage Arts and I show them pictures of the big fat crows that sit in our front yard back in the San Fernando Valley. Same kind of crows under the same sky 5000 miles apart.

All too soon it is time for me to take the train back. Lou walks me to the station. We laugh and we cuddle and we make plans to see each other again before another 40 years have passed. And I board the train grateful that the bacon man with excess saliva is nowhere to be seen. His digestive system is off on some other journey.

And as the train pulls out of the station, I marvel how we are each of us journeying somewhere, we just often forget to notice.

If your travels take you to Gourock, pop into Crow Cottage Arts. Say hello to Lou and Alec. And tell them Lynn from the Valley says Hi.

Sep 17, 2023

THE RIGHT PLACE

I can't believe I'm writing this but I suspect I may be allergic to Irn Bru. If you don't know what Irn Bru is, it's a bright orange magical pick-me-up in soda form. It's particularly Scottish and represents childhood parties, recovering from hangovers, and fish and chips suppers.

Anywhere you might have a coke, replace that coke with Irn Bru and it's miles better.

In fact, whenever I hear of a person who drinks too much coke, I shake my head sympathetically and think, "That poor soul has undoubtedly never tasted Irn Bru."

But it seems I must admire it from a distance.

The seasons are changing here in Scotland and I feel it. In a couple of days time, I'm leaving and heading back to the Valley where Mark and the boys, Arthur, and the chickens await.

I am ready to go. I have truly loved my time here in Scotland, but I ache for the space that is mine.

I worked with a guy many many moons ago on some commercial. I can't remember what it was we were advertising, but I remember we spent an inordinate amount of time sipping tea and Irn Bru in the green room waiting for the client to approve the lights/set/director.

Anyway, he was an older actor who was playing an even older man, and hence had the look of some kind of ancient wizard. He hailed from Aberdeen in the North East of Scotland and was very effusive about what a magical place it was. He claimed the dawn light on the grey granite buildings gave the city the air of being built in solid silver.

"But doesn't it get awful cold there? I'd asked.

"Aye," he'd replied, "But not such a cold that a warm fireside can't lift."

"And isn't it windy?" I'd said

"Oh, from time to time," he'd replied, "But then again, there's nothing like a brisk walk along the Queens Links to blow the cobwebs from a cluttered mind."

I'd sipped my Irn Bru and considered.

"I do think it's beautiful, but I don't think I could live there." I'd said.

"And that is the point," he'd exclaimed, "We are each of us tasked with finding the place we are happy- the place we were destined to be. I am lucky and from a very early age, knew that place to be Aberdeen. But not every traveler has such luck. Many folk will travel years and still not find the place they belong."

I was pondering this wisdom and was about to reply, when a head popped around the door and we were called to set to advertise whatever it was - electric blankets, or potato chips, or radiators.

And the moment had gone.

But his theory stayed with me: Maybe the journey of life is about finding happiness and searching for the place you belong.

Over this past couple of months I have discovered my belonging is not to a geographical place, it is with people. I love Scotland. I always will. I have slipped back into life here like into a favorite pair of slippers.

But my true happiness has been in taking up conversations with people that an ocean, and sometimes decades, have kept apart, with an ease that feels like family. Each of us living different lives, but with similar hopes and often similar challenges, always under the same sky.

If I met with the guy from the advert all those years ago, who I'm guessing is no longer here (unless he truly is a wizard) I know what I'd ask: "Is it possible that after traveling, you could find happiness in just being? "

I suspect he'd sip his tea, shrug and then reply that the answer to my question would lie solely within myself. Then maybe he'd ask why I wasn't drinking Irn Bru and I'd tell him it didn't agree with me. Then before he added any mystical context to that, I'd bore him with details of my gluten intolerance and my violent reaction to sorghum. Because some things just are.

Love has no distance. Life has no spreadsheet Irn Bru really is better than coke but that doesn't mean you can have it forever. Magic is everywhere. Even in Aberdeen. But belonging comes from the heart, not from Geography.

And so I return to the Valley, to my loud chickens, to a wee dog who believes I've vanished, to my giant growing sons, and to a human who is always where I belong.

Sep 24, 2023

BACK TO BASICS

Plus two cans of gin and tonic and a gluten-free pork pie.

I don't mind flying - by that I mean in a plane. I've never tried the other variants and considering the intense fear of heights I discovered I had when Mark and I thought about buying a lighthouse (a story for another day) I don't reckon I'll be trying any one of them soon.

Airports, I don't love. The endless queues, the plastic overpriced food, and the constant nagging feeling that if you don't keep your head together you could be in trouble. But the actual flying machines themselves, I'm good with.

Generally, I get in my seat. Get my headphones on. Stick my head in a book or the in-flight entertainment. I nod off for a bit, and then uncurl myself at the other end.

I check in as much baggage as possible so when people are wrestling over space in the overhead lockers, I smile a sympathetic smile. It's a system that works.

But as with every system, there's a day when it fails. Like it did this week when I traveled back from Scotland to LA.

The flight from Glasgow to London only lasts an hour, but this week there was an extra 3 hours in faff, delays, concourse busses, broken escalators, and more concourse busses. This meant that I arrived at gate security for the LA flight half an hour before take-off, which seemingly was way too late and I was not allowed on.

I wasn't alone. There was virtually a whole plane load of people transferring from different feeder flights who weren't allowed on, and the 'customer service' desks at American Airlines and British Airways were stacked.

It has to be said while the invention of the airplane undoubtedly illustrates the ability of humankind to achieve magnificence, British Airways customer service at Heathrow undoubtedly displays the opposite. One official seemed to equate service with screaming commands at people. The way she yelled in the face of an elderly couple made me feel sick to my stomach. But I guess in a competitive world, even psychopaths need to earn a living.

Anyway, the upshot of the flight delays was that I had the choice of sleeping overnight on the airport concourse or staying at an airport hotel.

Ever since I was a kid when I arrived at an airport, I'd look at the hotels and think, "What kind of idiot would stay in an airport hotel, when there's a whole world to explore?" Well it seems that every day is a learning opportunity. For though the entirety of London was there on my doorstep, it was late, I was exhausted and I just wanted the journey to be over. I was completely that kind of idiot and the hotel by the airport won.

Showered and dressed in an oversized t-shirt from British Airways overnight pack helpfully slung at me at the airport, I sat on the bed, the entirety of my possessions laid out in front of me.

Phone. Purse. Headphones. Charger. Hairbrush, toothbrush, toothpaste. Book. Chewing gum. Hand sanitizer.

Fortunately, I'd managed to find a Mark's & Spencer on the way to the hotel and picked up provisions presuming - accurately as it turned out -that any hotel next to an airport that changed 300 quid for their cheapest room would expect a second mortgage for any form of dinner.

I laid my bounty out in front of me: a big bottle of water, one banana, two cans of gin and tonic (necessary), a small tub of tomato and mozzarella salad, and incongruously, a gluten-free pork pie. All - well most - of the major food groups right there.

Yet actually after the day I'd had, I felt ridiculously grateful: To be clean, to be safe, to have food and a warm bed, everyone should be so lucky. If I could have thrown in a change of clothes for the next day, my life would have been complete.

But even then, I figured that was less my problem than the person unlucky enough to sit next to me on the plane the following day.

It crossed my mind about how when I'm writing a show, I never have any more props that I actually need. In order to get by the prop test, that item has to be vital.

But in life I carry so much stuff. And really how much do I need? I've been living with two suitcases of possessions for the past six weeks. Maybe when I do eventually get home, I could shed what I don't use anymore. Sometimes in life, it's time to lighten the load.

The next day I got on a plane to Los Angeles with renewed gratitude for the invention of flying machines. I was especially amenable to the people sitting next to me, only to discover they'd been bumped from their flight too - ah British Airways you rapscallion! They'd spent the night in a shitty hotel in central London, but were too tired to go out and see anything. I laughingly commented that we might be the stinkiest row of the plane, but they didn't even crack a smile so I took that as the cue to put on my headphones and dive into the in-flight entertainment.

I've now been back home for three days and I have changed my clothes more than a few times and unpacked my suitcases and my jet lag is subsiding nicely. But the desire to clear more space hasn't left.

It's good to take a moment to look at what you have and what really matters. Even when you don't really want to. There's a lot to be said for really noticing that you're warm, and safe, and have food, and a place to sleep. And all the other stuff that stresses you is just stuff and can wait till tomorrow.

The boys have been living quite happily while I've been gone, so I feel it would be a little out of order to come in like some house-clearing tornado. At least for this first week back. But it's coming. I don't need to keep everything I've been given. Some things can be let go.

In spite of British Airways Customer Service Heathrow, I do still believe travel broadens the mind. Even when I'm part of the stinkiest row on the plane.

Oct 1, 2023

ADULTING.

I'm back in LA this week and that means it's time to be up to date with all things medical. It's an American thing - the way the health system is over here, the time to see doctors is driven more by when the health insurance companies decide and when your deductibles are low (hang on to that NHS tooth and nail, UK people.)

I'm not generally a fan of going to the doctor's. This could be to do with that I don't really like being prodded and poked about, or that I'm not keen on the idea that I need help, or that my family doctor when I was a kid, would regularly do his consultations with a glass of whisky in one hand and a cigarette in the other. But I'm a big grown adult now, and I accept that part of being a big grown adult is that you have to do stuff that you don't particularly like.

The first time I walked into an oncologist's office I burst into tears. I'd just been diagnosed and had no idea what to expect, and there was a whole snafu with health insurance that meant I went to the oncologist rather than the surgeon first, because the primary doctor didn't know what he was dealing with. I could have been angry but I was too frickin scared. I cried mostly because there was no avoiding why I was there. I had to acknowledge I was now a member of "The Club That Nobody Wants To Join."

But that was a long time ago. And, honestly my attitude has changed.

During the Pandemic I found the Oncologist's strangely restful. Everybody in there had already considered their mortality. It was not a surprise. And in lockdown, people in real life had sort of had to hide themselves away like chemo patients - without the discomfort of actual chemo - which had a sort of camaraderie to it. So, while on the outside world, people were losing their shit, in the Oncologist's office everything felt pretty much like business as usual.

Every time I visit, I want to say to the women who come in crying like I first did, that the time where they were definitely going to die is over. Now they have an even chance. The scariest dance with cancer is when you don't know you have it. Knowing it feels worse, because everyone gets scared, but actually it's the beginning of the solution. But I shut my face. They're on their own journey and already have more than enough people with opinions in there.

Generally with those of us in past or current membership of The Club That Nobody Wants To Join, there's an acceptance that not everything really is within your control and it's a good idea to come to terms with that.

Outside people might talk about 'the battle' or 'the brave fight'. Inside people tend to be just getting on with it, because they understand the possibilities and they're not ready to die.

My disease is now classified as 'stable' (oncologists don't really do 'cured') which means that I am mind-blowingly lucky, and also that though I used to visit the oncologist every three months for blood work, now I've graduated to four.

Beside me in the waiting room, a figure bundled in a hoodie and pajamas lies almost lifeless over a bank of chairs. The man on the other side coughs behind his mask like his chest might explode. But in the chairs opposite, two women with headscarves chat animatedly about kids and birthdays and what they might be planning for Halloween.

I'm friendly with the staff there, and one of the bosses who once upon a time held my hand while I sobbed uncontrollably because I was in pain and terrified, saw me as I headed into an exam room.

'Hey,' he called out.

'Oh hi,' I said.

"What are you doing here?" he asked.

"Oh, you know me. I like to be where it's happening."

He laughed.

"You look great." he said.

"Thank you," I said. "You too."

"Honestly, you look kinda like you don't really belong here."

He smiled. I smiled too. A moment of unspoken understanding.

"Thank you," I said again. "For everything."

He nodded. "Meh," he said, and headed off.

The blood work looked good. I agree to come back again in 4 months, though soon we'll make it 5.

Back in the waiting room, the figure lying on the chairs has disappeared. In her place sits a tearful young woman, a small boy beside her playing with a toy truck and a mini Spiderman. I am mindful to keep out of their business. I don't need to know which one has joined the club.

I wave goodbye to my friend on reception. She wishes me Happy Holidays knowing I won't be back till after New Year.

And I am good. Occasionally I might find myself crying in a grocery store because of a song they're playing. Or I freeze when I think of someone who made me laugh and I suddenly remember they're no longer here. Or I notice my reflection in the mirror of some restaurant bathroom and I can't bear to look at the person I see. They tell me it's a form of survivor's guilt and it will ease.

From time to time I sit myself down and I have a cup of tea and remind myself that I'm a big grown adult, and that part of being a big grown adult is having to deal with stuff you don't fucking like. And I get over myself.

There is a club. Nobody wants to join it. And Nobody gets the choice. But if you're lucky - very very lucky - you get to put your membership on hold. That's a good thing to remember. Always. It helps to keep priorities in place.

SAY WHAT YOU MEME

Full confession. Sometimes when I read those peace-loving inspirational quote things on social media, I want to punch the writer in the face. And yes, I know that's hypocritical because I do myself periodically verge into the bigger-picture perspective, but that does not mean in any way I'm also not an asshole.

It is in our nature to be the hero of our own stories, but that still won't stop me showing up in other people's narratives as the villain or the fool.

There's been a building site across the street from us that's been going on for a while now - by a while I mean, over a year. The rumbling and house shuddering and 'this vehicle is reversing' noises would be annoying enough, but what's twice as annoying is that the foreman is not only not a people person, but a complete idiot. This has meant that they often have to repeat stuff that they've screwed up. They've drilled through a water main, and the gas main and I dread to think what they might do with the electricity. They've dug up the road outside or house more than a handful of times and regularly block off the whole street with big truck/small penis vehicles.

They're tricky to talk to because they seem to see being female as some sort of sub-class, and more than once I have to bite my lip so as not to say, ' If you're so fucking manly maybe get a pair of trousers to fit you properly."

218

They laugh in the face of regulations, but they weren't laughing this week when at 6 a.m., one of them started jackhammering just across from my bedroom window.

I'm not good when my sleep is disrupted, and especially not good when my sleep is disrupted by some jerk with a jackhammer. I was out there all hoodies and pajamas with my half-crumpled, old-lady face spouting - in full force Scottish accent - a tirade of expletives (which I call Gaelic if I'm ever challenged on it). As a result, I had managed to terrify a wee cluster of guys with massive tool belts, and call up the city to lodge a noise complaint before the clock even hit 7 am.

When my youngest got up and ready for school and wanted to talk to me about his 'problematic' English teacher, I had to say to him, "Son, I'm not at my parenting best this morning. I'm only on my first cup of tea and I've already been outdoors for a fight with some construction workers"

"And it's not even a Tuesday," he said.

"I know, but it is one of those days.'

"Oh," he said knowingly. Then he gave me a brief hug and said, "You'll be OK."

If you know me, you'll know I have a thing about Tuesdays. I believe that if anything shitty happens, it generally happens on a Tuesday. It's not a weird thing. It's statistics. So on Tuesdays we give ourselves more space, because anything might happen.

But a Tuesday scenario is totally different from a full-blown ' one of those days."

Because some days are just tricky. Sometimes it's because of circumstance. Sometimes you might get terrible news and not know how to process it. Sometimes there is no reason and you've just gotten out of the wrong side of bed. Other times, you get out of the right side of the bed but an hour and a half early -AGAIN -because of some complete jerk with a jackhammer.

On one of those days, I tend to work by the slogan "Do no harm to yourself or others."

Because on a particularly tricky day, my aim is to just try not to do something that I'll later regret: Don't get a face tattoo. Don't run away and try to join a circus. Don't yell at your accountant/dentist/ annoying lady in the shop. On one of those days when you hypothetically open a kitchen cupboard and a pack of badly placed crackers falls out and knocks a jar of badly placed Nutella off the countertop onto your bare feet, and really really hurts your toe, don't lose your shit about people not clearing up after themselves, and how you're the only person who ever takes one single moment to consider other people.

Instead, hop over to the kettle, make a cup of tea and resolve that tomorrow when the dust has settled, you can remind everyone about the cleaning up after themselves even when in a hurry rule.

"Do no harm to yourself or others" basically covers the vast grey area that lies between your bog-standard fairly difficult Tuesday, right up until 'go hide in your bed until this shitstorm is over'. Because it's fair enough to be pissed off at a day, but you don't want that day to become one that you particularly remember.

So that means when your youngest talks to you about his problematic English teacher, and you're still in full conflict with a construction worker mode, you don't respond with frustration to something that might need a bit of gentle care.

On days when I am doing no harm to others or myself, you might find me head down doing a jigsaw, or Goddamit knitting knick-knacks or whatever. When I was in Scotland my sister gave me a pattern for knitted birds, and I took it gratefully. I couldn't ever foresee a time when I might need an actual knitted bird, but I could foresee a time when I might need to knit one.

And the day passed and another day began and after a couple of proper uninterrupted nights' sleep, the rest of the week did improve. There were no knitted birds. There were no jigsaws. I had a bit of a clear-out and took stuff to the charity shop and there was a 76 lb pumpkin from the backyard that had to be made into puree. And then life went back to normal.

And later on in the week I went to my youngest's Back To School Night and met the 'problematic' English teacher.

I'm not at all surprised he gets her on a Tuesday.

Oct 15, 2023

NATURE.

Mark and I have been trying to work out why Arthur has been so over-exuberant of late. For a 7-year-old dog, he's behaving much more like a puppy. He's feisty and opinionated and very persistent in his pursuit of snacks. He's a little full-on.

We wondered that maybe it was down to the new glut of pumpkin puree in his food. (It's been a bumper year for pumpkins and they have to go somewhere.) Or maybe it's that he's on fancy vitamins to help his rickety old joints (because he used to periodically limp, and now he positively trots like that wee deer from the Babycham advert) We've not been able to work out what's going on with him, and then when we were out walking the other night, the thought crossed our mind: Maybe he's just happy.

I am Arthur's person. Though it was Lachlan who picked Arthur out at the Rescue, since the moment he placed his furry wee paws in our home, I am his go-to human. He struggled when I was away in the UK, and though it's possible to catch up with people through Zoom when there's a distance between you, it's not at all possible with dogs. Even the chickens had some sense of catch-up when they heard my voice on Zoom and came running for snacks (though Genghis did sulk a bit with me when I returned) but for Arthur it was all just confusing and made him more disorientated.

As a result, when I actually did come back home, Arthur was subdued. He was different, remote. I thought he might even have been slightly depressed. A new haircut and a week of almost normality and he was back to himself. And now, he is ridiculously perky and looks younger than he ever did.

It's been an interesting week for Mark too, as he won second prize for honey at the Annual San Fernando Valley Hive competition. It was completely out of the blue and crazily unexpected. It was a pretty big competition and he's only been a beekeeper for two years. But he does love his bees and they seem in return to love him - I say that not because other people judge their honey to be spectacular, but because of how improbably restful it is to watch one grown man and 40,000 wee stingy creatures co-exist when he's checking out their hive.

We got the hive when Russia invaded Ukraine. We felt so fucking powerless and wanted to do something but couldn't think what we could do. But we knew the world needs bees, so Mark built the hive. We didn't think about the honey. Only about the desire to do something positive. And that has seemed so incredibly relevant this week.

I've found it almost impossible to shake off my feelings of sorrow. I can't even look at the news. I don't want to hear smart-suited pundits explain the whos and the wheres. I don't want to listen to designer-clad Satanic Barbies mouth off on how this is a 'great opportunity' for members of any political party. I don't want to hear it explained or justified, because murdered children of any religion has to be unacceptable. My heart fucking aches for those who are involved. The brazen out-of-the-blue brutality makes me feel sick to my stomach. And I feel as powerless as Arthur.

Trying to find some semblance of understanding, I sat watching Mark with the bees. I considered that though there are some humans who seem to do their very best to destroy all that is good, Nature continues. Though there are plenty of homo sapiens who wish to express their dominance over all that is, the moon still decides on the turning of the tides, and the sun still controls when the dawn breaks.

Playing God does not make people Gods. They are not immortal. One day their own reckoning will come. They do not exist forever, and I will not give their mania a place in my head. I will mourn for the lives that were taken, not bow down to those who would steal those lives.

I have no answer. No explanation. I am as fucking useless as a dog on a Zoom call. But for those of you in pain, in fear, in grief, in horror, I see you. I think of you. I stand with you. I offer you love.

And in my sorrow and powerlessness, I lean into Nature. The giver and taker of all.

A WIG, A PROJECTOR, A KITE, A PANDA, AND A ROBOT.

15 years ago this week, Mark and I boarded a flight from the UK to California with our two sons – at that time aged 6 and 18 months old. The plan was that we were going to stay in America for three to six months, maybe a year.
We picked up 6-year-old, Ferg straight from school, so he was still in his school uniform, when we arrived - with all that we could pack into eight suitcases - in LAX on October 23rd, 2008.

Six weeks previously, I'd been offered a writing job at CBS. We lived in London. The job was in LA.
Time was tight. There was just enough time to pack up our life in London and find somewhere to live, but no time at all to organize all manner of other stuff you don't think about until you need it, like schools, and doctors, and driving licenses, and babysitters.

But sometimes all you really need to do in life is make the decision, and from there on in it's just negotiating details - admittedly in our case there were quite a lot of details, but details nevertheless.

Because we were so restricted with space, Mark and I limited ourselves to packing one 'luxury item' we could bring from the UK.

Mark, ever practical, brought a projector.

Fergus brought an Optimus Prime.

Lachlan brought 'Panda'.

I brought a wig and a kite. (Yes, I cheated. And yes, they're random. And yes, Freud might have had a field day, but Freud could frankly keep his opinions to himself as he wasn't trying to move two young kids across a continent.)

On Sunday, the day before I was due to start work, we got the keys to the house we'd rented from the internet. It had claimed to be part-furnished – but apparently in LA speak, 'part-furnished' meant that it had a cooker and a refrigerator: No beds, no sofa, no tables, no chairs, no crockery, no silverware, no sheets, no bedding.

Standing in the doorway of an almost empty house, suddenly 8 suitcases didn't seem like such a lot of stuff. And that's where I learned that IKEA do same-day deliveries. You know, it's easy to complain about IKEA with their randomly placed names and their mind-boggling assembly instructions, but as we settled down in our new incomprehensibly named beds in our new uncomfortably empty house on that first night, I announced that I'd never say a bad word against them again.

Mark - ever practical - said nothing. But we both agreed that though we'd just traveled 5000 miles, the largest part of the journey hadn't even yet begun.

And we were right. The following months were tricky: New job. New bank accounts. An out-of-state wedding. Then, on December 1st, my mother died.

Then, as if the year wanted to eke out as much stress as possible, the school lost my six-year-old in a public park after a Christmas concert. Thankfully we found him unharmed. We met with the school Principal to discuss the matter, She wanted to talk about my personal feelings - as if the issue was a matter of spirituality rather than safety. I have never felt more 'foreign' in my life.

Mark and I were perhaps a little "Braveheart' bordering on Shrek and Fiona. We explained that we were people who did take risks, but taking a risk is an entirely different thing from being completely fucking irresponsible.

Dignity almost intact, we quickly found our son another school where they at least would know where he was.

It really was the wildest white-knuckle ride.

Sitting in our barely furnished house on the last day of 2008, Mark and I could not believe how innocently the year had started, and we were frankly a little terrified as to what 2009 might bring.

And then we chilled out a bit and agreed that we were on an adventure and as with all good adventures, sometimes there are really frickin' scary bits. And also as we'd dealt with quite a lot of scary bits, surely the good stuff had to be on its way.

227

And it was. Periodically

There have been a fair amount of times in the past 15 years when something has happened and Mark and I have both taken a moment and said, "Well we did sign up for the adventure."

And there have been so many moments of brilliance too. I could never have imagined then that now I would be settled in old Tweddley Manor here in the Valley with Arthur and the chickens and the bees. There are so many wonderful people we have met that we wouldn't have known had we not stepped on that plane. And so so many reasons why I'm glad of the decision we made.

And as for our luxury choices: Yes, they were crazy. Yes, they were random. But in that first year, Mark's projector plugged into a laptop, meant we watched TV shows projected onto one of our big blank walls. Optimus Prime helped Fergus make one of his first new friends, Panda kept Lachlan company when he first went to daycare, and in my case, the wig had me fully prepared for my first American Halloween and the Kite was the perfect thing for the boys when we took them to the beach for the very first time.

So every year on October 23rd, we have a little party. Just the four of us with a cake and maybe a bit of pizza and we celebrate life, and choices, and Ikea same-day delivery. I still get a little freaked when I think back on it all. It was a lot. But given the chance would I do it all again? Oh hell, yeah.

WHAT IF YOUR INNER VOICE IS A JERK?

Years ago when I was in my early 20s and dinosaurs roamed the earth, I had surgery on my throat. Afterwards I was instructed, in no uncertain terms, to be silent - absolutely silent - for three weeks. (No talking, no muttering, no whispering).

Now I am a talker. I love a word or two or twenty or thirty or more. And if someone should ask me a question, I'm happy to get right in there with an answer. In fact, I'm happy to just have a chat whether a question was asked or not.

And back in those days when dinosaurs roamed the earth, I loved a good heated argument. But those were in the old pre-Trump days, when you didn't have to worry that the person you were arguing with, wouldn't turn out to be some pretty normal-looking conspiracy lunatic - Ah those halcyon days when full-blown crazy people would be more conveniently recognizable by wearing tin foil hats or the like.

Anyway, the point is that as a talker who could not talk, the only solution open to me was to give myself nobody to talk to. So, I retreated to a little Scottish island where I knew nobody, nobody knew me, to live out my three weeks of silence on my own.

The island in question was the Isle of Cumbrae just off the west coast of Scotland. It has one little town, Millport, where pretty wee souvenir stores, cafes, and cycle hire shops dot along the promenade. My Dad used to say that he believed that in good weather, it was the most beautiful place on Earth, and only a fool would disagree. On a clear day, you can see across the Clyde estuary to Ben Lomond, and in the Summer months, this tiny little island gives off an air of all being right in the world.

When I arrived for my self-enforced exile, it was October and the rain hammered down like glass rods.

Nevertheless, the first day was really quite lovely. The house was on the seafront. I put the fire on and read a book, occasionally glancing out the window to watch the waves dancing in the wind. When night came though, and there was nothing to see from the window but darkness, my troubles began.

It started in a small way as all the most terrifying things do, with a simple thought that muttered, "What if…?" in the dark recesses of my mind.

"What if you never talk again?" It said. "What would that be like?"

I didn't like the sound of that at all, so I pushed it out of my head.

"I mean, they've said it should be fine, but nothing in life is a given and they won't know for sure until after a month. There are no guarantees."

Again I pushed it out of my head…

Only for it to return like a bad smell.

"Because if you aren't able to talk again, think about all of the things you won't be able to do. Maybe you should prepare yourself."

"I'll be fine. I'd manage." I argued to myself.

A matter of point here: Arguments inside your own head are much more difficult to handle than arguments with full-blown tin-foil-hat-wearing crazy people, because, when it's a tin-foil-hat-wearing crazy person you can walk away when it gets too much, but when the crazy person is inside your own head, there is no escape.

"It's not all about you though, is it?" my asshole inner voice continued. "How about your family? How about your friends? How difficult would it be for them dealing with your brokenness? Think how much of a burden you'd become. How much of a burden you probably are already. Imagine."

"Uhm no. I don't want to imagine. Thanks, but I don't. For fuck's sake, it's only throat surgery. I am going to get better."

"'Oh really? This time last year, you didn't even know there was a problem with your throat. And look at you now. Just exactly how good are you at judging anything?"

And so it continued till the daylight hours, or until I was so tired of arguing in my head, I'd fall asleep exhausted.

And that is why at 3 am on the second night, though the rain still hammered down like glass rods, I stood on the shoreline, looking out to a sea so dark I could only sense it through the roar of the waves in the blackness. I was cold and wet and shivering but I didn't care. I thought if I could feel something physically, then I might be able to drown out the noise in my head.

I'd like to tell you that the next day things improved, but they did not. I lit the fire, took out my book, made cups of hot tea, but my mood would not lift. My sorrow hung around me like a dampness I couldn't shake off.

And I dreaded the night when the argument would begin again. "What if…? What if?"

One more matter of point: When it comes to arguments, some you win and some you lose. But when you're on your own in the middle of the night, suck it up, you are going to lose.

On the fourth day, I went for a walk during daylight hours. I'd been avoiding going out during the day as I was exhausted through lack of sleep and also I didn't want to bump into anyone and have to be silent. (Bad enough to not be able to talk to those who know you. Bloody impossible to try to explain to those you'd never met before.)

The rain had stopped. The sky was overcast. The clouds, heavy with the promise of another downpour. The seafront was deserted. But I could see the light from a little grocery/souvenir store someway in the distance. I thought about changing direction, knowing I should avoid people, but I didn't. Instead, I walked towards the store and looked in the window.

There was a daft wee display of novelty cups, a teddy bear with a kilt on, and a selection of little tartan notepads. I've always been a fan of the tartan, and the notepad that I wrote my 'emergency' "I'm sorry, I can't talk!" notes in was running low. So, I decided to treat myself.

Through a series of polite smiles and nods, I was able to conduct the business of buying the notepad, but instead of buying the little tartan one, I bought a full-fat A4-sized, lined notepad.
I took it back to the house, made myself a cup of tea, sat down and I wrote.

I wrote a list of things I wanted to do. Things I was sorry I hadn't done already. People I wanted to say sorry to. Things I wanted to forgive myself for. I wanted so much to stop the argument.

I set out how I was going to change my life. I wrote about what I would say if I could speak and who I would speak those words to.

And when the darkness came and the 'what ifs' started again, I wrote a list of those little fuckers down on paper too so that I could attend to them when or if I ever needed to, rather than let them run riot in my head. And afterward, for the first time since the surgery, I slept a solid 10 hours.

Up until then, whenever I'd written anything, it was mannered - like every word on the page had to please someone else: a schoolteacher, a college lecturer, some imaginary critic I'd installed in my head. Like writing was some form of dressage I had to train myself for in a competition.

But there was no place for any of that in my self-enforced exile. Just me, my A4, and my pen.
So, the fire burned in the hearth and the rain poured outside, and the waves roared in the darkness, I wrote and I slept and I wrote and I slept, and then it was time to return home.

Back at the hospital, the doctors were very very pleased with my recovery. They asked how I'd managed with the three weeks of silence. I said nothing and gave them a winning smile. I was given a clean bill of health and the freedom to go enjoy my life, with the instruction of no shouting or singing for a while.

And obviously my speaking voice completely repaired, although there are days I'm sure not everybody sees this as a great advantage.

Though this happened such a long time ago - (I was in my early 20s and dinosaurs were roaming the earth) the lessons I learned took up residence in my head and gave most of the 'what ifs' their eviction orders.

I learned that fear will always be a close companion when I am going through any form of change. And I learned not to pay far too much attention because the whole point of existence is change.

I know how much I need people, even though that annoys me, because frankly some of them are assholes.

I like to think I can handle everything on my own, but, truthfully, at precisely the time when it feels like the hardest thing in the world would be to talk to someone, that's exactly the time when I know I absolutely should.

I try not to get into arguments with myself. As I know all my own weak spots I can be fairly brutal, and frankly my inner voice can be a pessimistic, belligerent, cruel fucking jerk.

Life can be tough. Sometimes through no willful fault of your own, you can find yourself cold and shivering looking out into nothing but the roaring darkness.
I know that feeling when your inner voice is kicking your ass and nobody can hear you, and you can't see the future.

Just as I know -to my very core- that when I find myself grieving for all I have lost, I am literally on the brink of some incredible beauty yet to be found.

And also I miss the days when fully-fledged, bat-shit-crazy lunatics had the civility to wear full-blown, tin-foil hats.

A SERENITY GARDEN FFS

I live in a house in Van Nuys with three boys, one dog, nine chickens, and 40,000 bees, so even the idea of being "nestled amidst the calm" of anything frankly is a little out there. (There are times when I've yelled from behind the toilet door, 'Leave me alone. I'm allowed to be in here. It's my biological right. It's part of the Geneva Convention!")

And that's why I found myself wanting a Serenity Garden. (I know, I can't believe it either. I'm from Cumbernauld.)

But, you see a Serenity Garden is an "indoor or outdoor space where you grow a couple of plants - trees if you can- and maybe some flowers. And in this tranquil place, you can kick back from the world and daydream, or meditate, all the while being nestled amidst the calm wonder of Nature."

And ever since I heard that, I've bloody wanted one.

It could have been argued that I already had a quiet space where I could cut myself off from the world and contemplate - but Serenity Toilet doesn't have the same ring.

Anyway, one day I came out of my office after quite a harrowing session with a story client.

In my day job, I work to help people uncover the stories of their lives: sometimes to write them, other times just to help them understand them. Some people have really really tough things they're dealing with, and that particular session had been a corker.

Afterwards, I'd stood in the backyard making myself breathe slowly, trying to dampen my rage, staring at the sky waiting for the Universe to explain how when it comes to pain, loss, and difficulty, the cards don't appear to be dealt out equally.

Mark, familiar with the pose, had appeared from the kitchen and asked in a low tone, "Are you alright?" To which I replied, "No. I need a fucking Serenity Garden."

He understood. So we built one on a wee patch of garden. Roses. Some succulents. A bay tree. A wee citrus tree. And a little fountain I got off Craigslist for $50.

It's lovely. And it is serene. But it's not called a Serenity Garden. It's called, "The Fucking Serenity Garden," and that seems to suit me better somehow.

I curse and swear. Sometimes it's because I'm angry. Sometimes because I'm sad. Or because I'm surprised, or amazed, or happy too. I would say for me that the word, 'fuck' is probably the little black dress of vocabulary - there is not an occasion to which it doesn't quite fit.

I'm aware that I'm meant to be ashamed about that, but I'm fucking not.

If I said, "Oh duck," it would be fine. People would smile knowingly at the naughty word I could have said, but cleverly avoided. I would be considered witty rather than uncouth.

And it's literally just one letter difference. The fact is, depending on which consonant you pick up either side of the letter e can determine whether you have a filthy mouth or a basic understanding of ornithology.

Of course, there's a time and a place and everything. Like I wouldn't use it at my kid's Parents' Evening or at a 5-year-old's birthday party. I wouldn't write it in a piece of 'family entertainment.'

But if I'm talking frankly with you, there's a pretty good chance an F-bomb will slip out. Not because I want to offend you, not because I think it's big or clever, just because somewhere in my psyche it is the little black dress of vocabulary.

And I know that it's not for everybody.

There's a lady in Scotland who comes to shows of mine so she can hate them - and I'm not even kidding. During the show, she'll sit in the audience and tut when I swear. Sometimes she'll mutter phrases like "Your mother would be disgusted if she heard you talk like that" which wholeheartedly assures me that this woman really didn't know my mother at all.

My mother wanted me to talk from the heart. To be honest. To see the joy in things. To laugh. To challenge myself. She didn't love that I used the f-word, but she wasn't that keen on me bleaching my hair either. My Mother and I were good.

Anyway, I don't know how many times this woman has come to see my shows - but definitely a few. My heart always sinks when I spot her angry face in an audience because I have to be mindful not to pick on her or to single her out. My mother tolerated my language but she was uncompromising on the need to be compassionate and kind.

During one show, I found myself wondering why anyone would repeatedly pay to come and see a performer who annoyed them so much. Like, did she think I would improve? Evidently she has a story going on in her head that I'm not a party to. For that I am glad. I don't really want to hear her story. I expect if I did, I'd be standing out in the backyard raging at the Universe about unfairness. I am sorry she is not a happy person, but she does not get to dictate who I am.

Sometimes this woman will complain to my face after the show. More often than not, she'll complain to someone else, maybe grab a hold of an usher, or announce something loudly at the bar. She tells everyone she is very disappointed in me. I haven't the heart to tell her that I too am often terribly disappointed in me.

But not for fucking swearing.

Look, I'm not saying there aren't some words that don't make me wince. Collateral for example. That's not a word I like. You could even change a couple of consonants in there and it's still not going to improve. It's a bad word. It says bad things.

Armed. I don't like that either. I try and cheer it up in my head by thinking of it as being defined as an octopus doing jazz hands and that seems to help.

Offensive - I don't like that either as an adjective or a noun. Offensive is, as it clearly states, offensive.

When I hear all three words together in the same sentence, well, that's enough for me to beat the retreat to my Fucking Serenity Garden and try to nestle amidst the fucking calm.

It's developed a bit since we first built it. The bay tree has grown and is now taller than me. Roses bloom in shades of red and pink and peach and white. The wee citrus tree is considering bearing fruit, and a small patch of lavender attracts the bees. We've moved the $50 fountain to another part of the yard, and it's been replaced by a bust of Julius Caesar someone gave me as they wanted rid of it, and I've spray-painted it gold.

But it's not always perfect. Periodically, someone in the house may call out, "Arthur is peeing in The Fucking Serenity Garden again." And I may look out the window and tut and shake my head. And I may notice that Arthur actually looks like he's smiling while he's doing it. And I may comment loudly how "that sort of stuff wouldn't happen in a proper serenity garden." And then I shrug, and I chuckle, because me and that garden are both a long long way from proper.

Nov 12th, 2023

BRICK. PAPER. SCISSORS.

In our old house, there was a weird little wall right next to the refrigerator in the kitchen. It had dates and names and heights written on it.

We started it when the kids were little, and we wanted to see how much they were growing, and we thought that the perfect place to mark their heights would be this little wall.

So they'd stand up straight with their backs against the wall and we'd balance a pencil on the top of their heads and then mark off on the wall their heights and the date. It was sweet.

But then the kids wanted to see how tall they were in comparison to everyone else, so Mark and I put our own heights up there as well.

Before long, just about everyone who came into the house stood to have their height measured: The neighbors. The kids' school friends. The kids' school friends' parents. The cleaning lady. The cleaning lady's daughter. Everyone who came to film in the studio. Performers. Producers. Tradespeople. Writers. My niece, visiting from Scotland. My nephew. Cousins, Aunties, Uncles, and Friends of over 20 years – all stood to have their heights marked up on this daft little wall.

At one point, the wall was almost impossible to read in places because it was so cluttered with names, heights, and dates. (Who knew we knew so many people between 5'4 and 5'9?)

And then the house was remodeled. And the wall was painted over. And then it was just a plain, odd, little blank wall next to the refrigerator. And it was fine. And stylish. Very stylish. And the kitchen looked like a grown-up's kitchen. Clean. Plain. Tidy. And really very nice.

But something was missing. Because houses are just shells without people. Walls without memories are just rows of brick.

So we started again.

New names and heights and dates went up. And as they did, I could kind of remember where some of the old heights were. I had the new list written on the wall in front of me, and the old list written somewhere in the back of my mind. Sometimes when I walked into the kitchen I would laugh passing the wall, as some random vision of someone who had once stood against it, came to mind.

And if I stopped for just a minute, I could recall scenes like old home movies: My youngest cheering when he spotted he was almost as tall as his Aunty. My eldest guffawing when he was taller than his father, and boasting that now he was not only taller but he had more hair. Two fully grown adults visiting from abroad arguing about who might have been "cheating" because one was surprisingly taller than the other. A friend brushing her hand against the wall with a faint melancholy smile, seeing the name and height and date of someone who once was.

Occasionally, I would just sit and look at the list on the wall, and allow the memories of all the silliness to come roaring back. Christmases and Birthdays and good days and bad days. Family dinners and arguments and packed lunches and Halloween costumes. Holding onto my eldest as he cried over the unfairness in the world. All four of us laughing when my youngest announced that if his father had special powers, it would be that he could sense if there was a Home Depot anywhere in the area. There could be Spiderman, Batman, and HomeDepotMan.

But life is a sequence of letting go. We moved on. We are not as we were. We no longer live in that house.

When the developer who bought the house called to say that it was soon to be demolished, and asked if there was anything else we wanted to take, I thought of the list on the wall, and found myself unreasonably tearful. Not because of the bricks and mortar – although sort of completely because of the bricks and mortar.

Though houses are just shells without people, walls full of so many memories lie in simple rows of bricks.

When I was the age my kids were when we started that wall, I couldn't wait for time to pass. I felt like days – especially school days – lasted forever, and I remember always being furious on Christmas night that I was going to have to wait a whole other year before Christmas came again.

But now, at my full height, I don't feel that way anymore. Christmas feels like it's barely finished before another one begins. Time sped up somewhere along the line. My babies are not babies anymore. Too many of the names written on the wall are no longer here.

And Ok, so life is a sequence of letting go. But what if you don't want to let go?

Where we live now, there is no wall to write heights on. And nobody needs measured. My kids are tall and very tall, and Mark and I suspect we're getting shorter.

A year ago, I sat down one Sunday and wrote a little blog, and sent it out into the Universe.

And I felt better.

So I did it again the next Sunday.

And as I wrote, all the little stories came back in my head in clear bright technicolor. And each blog felt a bit like marking a name and a date and a height on a daft wee wall next to a refrigerator. So I carried on sending them out.

In the end, all of our moments travel into the mists of the past, to a place where once vibrant memories dissolve.

But for me, these little blogs are like snapshots. Daft wee postcards, delivered along the way. Sent as a reminder of how the world once looked and what once was. Small and insignificant, lofty and blundering, proud, fearful, cheerful, shy. Just like names, heights, and dates marked on a wall next to a refrigerator.

So I wrote this book and it's much more convenient to transport than plasterboard and bricks.

THANK YOU

Paul Sullivan for all-round braininess and efficiency.

Fiona Francois for swankiness and generosity.

Ashley Forbes with whom I share so many stories.

Maryanne Restivo for laughs, mischief, and keeping my secrets.

Janice and Eddie McCann for their creative couch in Cumbernauld.

Those who freely offered words of kindness: Catherine Burns, Chesney Hawkes, Gavin Mitchell, and Alfred Molina.

And to you out there reading this book and those blogs.

You are beautiful people, one and all.

ABOUT THE AUTHOR

Lynn Ferguson is a self-confessed Entertainment Mongrel hailing from the picturesque Scottish hamlet of Cumbernauld in Scotland. Writer, performer, and all-round show-off, she now lives in the San Fernando Valley in California with her husband, Mark Tweddle, and two sons Fergus and Lachlan. They have one dog, Arthur, 10 chickens, and about 40000 bees.

Lynn is most likely to be known for her voice as 'Mac' in the Chicken Run movies, but also known for her theatrical plays, one-woman shows, and TV appearances. She has awards and other accolades but she always changes the subject if you ever mention them.

Printed in Great Britain
by Amazon

32488028R00142